My First
Catholic
Bible

is presented to

Given by

Date

Occasion

A Special Letter to Children
from
Mother Teresa of Calcutta

+LDM   6 May 1997

My dear Children

God loved the world so much that He sent us His only Son to
save us from sin. And Jesus brought us the Good News that
God loves each one of us with a most tender love. We are
precious to Him. He has carved us in the palm of His hand.
And we are created for greater things: to love and to be loved.

It is so important for us to know the Word of God. Because if
we know it, we will love it; and if we love it, we will keep it
and live it. Let us ask Mary, the Mother of Jesus and our
Mother, for the grace to imitate her. She kept the Word of
God and pondered it in her heart. And to be able to do that,
we must pray. Prayer gives a clean heart, and a clean heart
can see God and know His will for us.

Jesus tells us, "Love one another as I have loved you."
And how do we do that? Love begins in the family. I begin
by loving my father and my mother, my brothers and sisters;
my friends in the neighbourhood and at school and all those
I meet in my town or city. Love to be true must hurt, must
cost us something. When we love like that, ready to make a
sacrifice, we will find peace and joy.

Look around and see if there is anyone around you who is sick,
poor, lonely, or feeling unloved or unwanted. We don't have
to do big things. What counts is that we do small things with
great love - giving a smile, a kind word, a helping hand,
bringing a glass of water, sharing a sweet. Remember that we
do it to Jesus because He said, "Whatever you do to the least,
you do it to Me." So let us pray much that we may be the
sunshine of God's love to all we meet.

Let us pray.   *God bless you*
                                          M Teresa mc

My First Catholic Bible

New Testament Edition

Illustrated by Natalie Carabetta

Contemporary English Version

THOMAS NELSON PUBLISHERS

Nashville

About the Illustrator

Natalie Carabetta was born in Meriden, Connecticut, in 1963. She graduated from the Philadelphia College of Art in 1985 and has been illustrating books for children since 1990. Presently, Natalie lives in Perkasie, Pennsylvania, with her daughter, Grace.

Quotation Rights for the Contemporary English Version Bible

Contents

The Devotionals

(Use the boxes to the left of the Devotionals to check off the ones you've read.)

CONTENTS

Welcome to the
Contemporary English Version

Languages are spoken before they are written. And far more communication is done through the spoken word than through the written word. In fact, more people *hear* the Bible read than read it for themselves. Traditional translations of the Bible count on the *reader's* ability to understand a *written* text. But the *Contemporary English Version* differs from all other English Bibles—past and present—in that it takes into consideration the needs of the *hearer,* as well as those of the reader, who may not be familiar with traditional biblical language.

The *Contemporary English Version* has been described as a "user-friendly" and a "mission-driven" translation that can be *read aloud* without stumbling, *heard* without misunderstanding, and *listened to* with enjoyment and appreciation, because the language is contemporary and the style is lucid and lyrical.

The *Contemporary English Version* invites you to *read*, to *hear*, to *understand* and to *share*

the Word of God now
as never before!

Learn to Pray the Rosary

Now that you have your very own Bible, you can use it not only to learn the stories and memory verses, you can also use it to learn the Our Father and the Hail Mary. Then you will be able to pray the Rosary every day.

Below, you'll see that we have divided the prayers of the Rosary. Ask your parents or someone from your church to teach you how to use a Rosary and soon you will be able to pray it every day.

First, you can memorize one line each day for five days. Try doing this every morning while you eat breakfast or in the afternoons after school. You could even work on them while you're going to sleep at night. Some people seem to think better at certain times of the day, so just pick the time you're most alert and use it to memorize a line of a prayer.

Or, if you need to take a little longer, spend five days learning each line by breaking them into small sections and memorize a few words at a time.

Pretty soon, you'll be able to pray the Rosary all by yourself.

Our Father

Our Father who art in heaven, hallowed be thy name.

Thy kingdom come. Thy will be done on earth, as it is in heaven.

Give us this day our daily bread,

and forgive us our trespasses, as we forgive those
who trespass against us,

and lead us not into temptation, but deliver us from evil. Amen.

Hail Mary

Hail Mary, full of grace! The Lord is with thee,

blessed art thou among women,

and blessed is the fruit of thy womb, Jesus.

Holy Mary, Mother of God,

pray for us sinners, now and at the hour of our death. Amen.

Glory Be to the Father

Glory be to the Father,

to the Son, and to the Holy Spirit.

As it was in the beginning,

is now, and ever shall be,

World without end. Amen.

Introduction

Looking for a Best Friend?
We all need one. Someone we can share our secrets with. Someone who likes us. Someone who's fun to be around. We need somebody like that to talk to every day.

My First Catholic Bible, New Testament Edition, will help you become best friends with the *best* Best Friend of all—the wonderful God, creator of heaven and earth. God knows all about you, and he likes you very much. He loves you deeply. He's a joy to be with. You can tell him all your secrets. And you can spend time with him every day—for the rest of your life.

God becomes our Best Friend . . .

- when we ask Jesus Christ, his Son, to forgive our sins and to give us everlasting life, and . . .
- when we begin reading our Bibles and praying every day.

Daily Bible reading and praying is like talking with God himself. He speaks to us when we read his book, the Bible. And we speak to him when we pray. These daily times of Bible study and prayer make us more and more devoted to God, which is why we call them—daily devotions.

Here are seven ways to get the most from *My First Catholic Bible:*

1. Use it about the same time each day—maybe in the morning before school or at night just before going to bed.

2. Think of each day's passage as a special message from God just for you.

3. Study the pictures. Each has been drawn to accurately show something about the words you're reading.

4. Use the prayer starters to . . . well, to start your prayers. Then go on to tell God whatever you'd like. Learn to talk to him naturally, just like talking to a friend.

5. Work hard on the memory verses. Collect all of them in your mind.

6. Use weekends to look over Scriptures you've previously read and to review verses you've already learned.

7. If you *do* occasionally skip a day, make sure you don't miss the next one. Make your daily devotions a habit, and stick to them.

No matter how many—or how few—friends you have, you've got one Best Friend who will never leave you or let you down. And he's waiting for you to get to know him better . . . just as soon as you turn to page 16.

A Word for Parents

Deuteronomy 6.5-7 tells parents how to help their children get established in a lifestyle of daily prayer and Scripture reading. The order established in that passage is important. First, parents should love the Lord with all their hearts. Next we're to memorize his Word, his laws. Then we are to talk about them all the time to our children.

My First Catholic Bible, New Testament Edition, can help.

- For younger children, use this as a read-to-me picture book of daily devotions.

- For older children, gently monitor their use of this book and help them build the "daily devotional" habit into their routine.

- Keep your own copy of *My First Catholic Bible* (you can use it for your devotions, too) so you can talk more easily about the Scripture wherever you are and whatever you're doing.

- Provide a full copy of the *Bible* so your children can look up surrounding passages for further study.

- Help your child learn the memory verses. John Ruskin, English social critic, said the verses his mother helped him memorize in childhood "set my soul for life." Use charts, stars, incentives, and rewards. Make it a family project.

- Involve your family in a good church with a strong youth ministry.

- Be a spiritual model for your children. The best way to entice your kids into the daily devotional habit is to let them see you enjoying yours.

Our spiritual vitality depends on two aspects of victorious Christian living: conversion and conversation. The first is a matter of heart; the second, of habit. When we meet Christ at the cross, that's *conversion*. When we meet with him behind the closed door, that's *conversation*.

> *The message about **the cross** doesn't make any sense to lost people. But for those of us who are being saved, it is God's power at work (1 Corinthians 1.18).*

> *When you pray, go into a room alone and **close the door**. Pray to your Father in private. He knows what is done in private, and he will reward you (Matthew 6.6).*

We're converted to Jesus Christ when we trust him as Savior, confessing our sins to him, asking him for eternal life, and committing ourselves to him as Lord and Master. Then the friendship starts. The God of the Universe wants to meet us each day over an old Book at the kitchen table. It's beyond comprehension.

God is both infinite and intimate! He delights in being with his people, hearing us pray and talking to us through his Word. The Master, it seems, occupies two addresses: in the highest heavens and with the humblest hearts.

The heavenly Father wants our earthly friendship. Could anything be more astonishing than that?

Only one: many of us can't find time for him. We're too busy for Bible study, and too pooped for prayer.

We rush into each day, bolting from bed like a thoroughbred from the gate. We gulp down our coffee, throw on designer labels, then veer onto the fast lane. We whirl through our daily tasks like a spinning top, then drive by the restaurant on the way home so they can throw food to us through the window. We drag ourselves to the couch for an hour of video violence, then stagger to be bed for six hours of sleep. Whatever happened to green pastures and still waters? We're too frazzled to find them!

But suppose you do go to bed at a reasonable hour and get up a half hour earlier to meet God the next morning—what do you do with those thirty minutes? I'd like to suggest a sequence called *JARS and Rs.*

J=Jot

J stands for "jot." You'll need a notebook for this, but any kind will do. At the top of the page, jot the date. You can then write anything you want about your feelings, your moods, or the circumstances of your life. Or, just use the margin of your Bible to jot down the date and any useful information.

After you've written everything you want to remember, you're ready for the next step.

A=Ask

Take a moment to ask God to speak to you through his Word. Though some people read the Bible only as a textbook, it's primarily a love letter between the Lord and his people. It's designed to transform and invigorate our lives as the Holy Spirit applies it to our hearts. Ask God to open your mind to what he wants to teach you, and ask him to help you know what he wants you to do.

R=Read

Then read your Bible. Begin each day where you left off the day before. Underline significant phrases. Study cross-references. Diagram sentences. Outline chapters. Check key words in a dictionary. Dig into the text, looking for contrasts and comparisons. Rewrite verses in your own words in your notebook. There are no rules for where or how much to read. The important thing is remembering as you read that God is talking to you as one talks to a friend.

S=Select

As you study the Bible, look for one verse to select as your *verse-for-the-day*—a verse that really hammers at your heart. When you find it, copy it in your journal and perhaps on a scrap of paper to carry with you all day. I know one man who writes his verse on the back of a business card that he props on his desk. Another friend jots hers on a sticky note to post on her dashboard. She memorizes it as she drives to work.

Find your verse-for-the-day in the morning, carry it in your heart all day, and at night meditate on it as you fall asleep.

Then having listened to the Lord, it's time to speak to him. The last half of your quiet time centers around the three *Rs* of prayer.

R=Rejoice

Begin by rejoicing, praising, and thanking God for his grace and generosity. A good place to start is with your verse-for-the-day. Usually when engaged in conversation, I respond and react to the words of the one speaking to me. If he's talking about football, I don't abruptly begin a discourse on the excavations of Crocodilopolis. I follow the flow of the conversation.

If your verse-for-the-day is Matthew 22.37—*Love the Lord your God with all your heart . . .*—tell God how much you love him and thank him for his love for you. Rejoice that you have a love-based relationship with the Almighty.

R=Repent

As you worship the Lord, you may begin to feel inadequate, like Peter in Luke 5.8, who, amazed at Christ's miracle of fish, fell at his knees saying, *"Lord, don't come near me! I am a sinner."*

So we move naturally from rejoicing to repenting. We admit to God faults and failures we've knowingly allowed to mar our lives since we last prayed.

R=Request

Then we're ready to obey Philippians 4.6: *With thankful hearts offer up your prayers and requests to God.* The Lord promises to answer our prayers if we sincerely ask in the name of the Lord Jesus—with one condition inserted for our protection: He only promises to grant us those things that are good for us, that are according to his will (1 John 5.14-15).

So pray with confidence, using your journal to record your requests and to note God's answers. Pray aloud when you can, and talk to God naturally, as though speaking with a friend. Because you are.

Don't grow discouraged if sometimes you don't feel like praying. Pray anyway. Don't quit on mornings when you don't enjoy your Bible reading. Read anyway. Don't despair if you miss a day. Start again the next.

Develop the habit, then the habit will develop you. Cultivate the friendship, and your Friend will stick closer than a brother.

The impact on your children will be for keeps.

People You'll Meet in
My First Catholic Bible

Who in the world is Nicodemus? Barnabas? Sceva? Ever heard of Ananias and Sapphira?

These hard-to-say names belong to some very interesting people you'll meet in *My First Catholic Bible, New Testament Edition*. The following list can help you get to know them. Beside every name is a helpful guide to pronouncing it correctly, and a description of the person's identity. At the end of each entry you'll find the page number first mentioning that character.

Jesus *(GEE zus)* - the Son of God, the Savior of the world, who was both God and man (p. 16)

Herod *(HEHR ud)* - the king of Israel when Jesus was born (p. 16)

Mary *(MAIR ee)* - the wife of Joseph and the woman chosen by the Lord as the mother of Jesus (p. 17)

Joseph *(JOE zeph)* - a carpenter from Nazareth; the husband of Mary, mother of Jesus (p. 17)

Simon Peter *(SIGH mun PEE ter)* - a fisherman who was brought to Jesus by his brother Andrew; he became one of Jesus' apostles (p. 23)

James *(jamez)* **and John** *(jahn)* - the sons of Zebedee; fishermen who became apostles of Jesus (p. 26)

Pilate *(PIE lat)* - the Roman governor of Judea during the time of Jesus (p. 31)

Jairus *(jay EYE ruhs)* - a ruler of the Jewish meeting place whose daughter needed healing from Jesus (p. 34)

Pharisees *(FARE uh sees)* - the religious teachers of Jesus' day (p. 37)

Elizabeth *(ee LIZ uh buth)* - the cousin of Mary and the mother of John (p. 44)

John *(jahn)* - the son of Zechariah and Elizabeth; the man God sent to prepare the people to receive Jesus (p. 52)

Judas *(JOO duhs)* - the apostle who betrayed Jesus (p. 68)

Nicodemus *(nick oh DEE mus)* - a Pharisee and Jewish leader who came to Jesus at night (p. 77)

Mary *(MAIR ee)* **and Martha** (MAR thuh) - sisters from the town of Bethany; Jesus was a close friend of their family (p. 83)

Lazarus *(LAZ ah russ)* - the brother of Mary and Martha who was raised from the dead by Jesus (p. 83)

Mary Magdalene *(MAIR ee MAG deh leen)* a woman from Magdala of Galilee who was one of Jesus' most devoted followers (p. 91)

Ananias *(an uh NYE us)* **and Sapphira** *(suh FIGH ruh)* - a husband and wife who were struck dead for lying to the Holy Spirit (p. 104)

Stephen *(STEE vun)* - a man of great faith and filled with God's Spirit who was chosen by the twelve apostles to serve God (p. 110)

Simon *(SIGH mun)* - a man of Samaria who practiced witchcraft, but came to believe in Jesus (p. 113)

Philip *(FILL ihp)* - one of seven men chosen by the apostles to serve God by going from place to place telling the good news (p. 113)

Saul *(sawl)* - a man from the city of Tarsus who hated Christians until he came to know Jesus as his Savior; he later became known as Paul, a great preacher of the gospel (p. 115)

Paul *(pawl)* - a faithful follower of Jesus and an apostle to the Gentiles; he took the gospel throughout all the regions north of the Mediterranean Sea; he was originally known as Saul (p. 123)

Barnabas *(BAR nuh bus)* - a devoted follower of the Lord who sold all his goods to give to the work of Christ; he was known as the son of encouragement (p. 125)

Silas *(SIGH lus)* - a loyal companion and friend of Paul who went with him on one of his missionary trips (p. 130)

Timothy *(TIM uh thih)* - a faithful servant of the Lord who was like a son to Paul and served as his assistant (p. 131)

Aquila *(A kwil uh)* **and Priscilla** *(prih SIL uh)* - a Jewish couple who made tents for their living; followers of the Lord and friends of Paul (p. 138)

Sceva *(SEE vuh)* - a Jewish high priest whose seven sons tried to force out evil spirits by using the name of the Lord Jesus (p. 143)

Philemon *(fie LEE mun)* - a wealthy man who used his large house for church meetings (p. 181)

Wise Men from the East

When Jesus was born in the village of Bethlehem in Judea, Herod was king. During this time some wise men[a] from the east came to Jerusalem [2]and said, "Where is the child born to be king of the Jews? We saw his star in the east[b] and have come to worship him."

[3]When King Herod heard about this, he was worried, and so was everyone else in Jerusalem. [4]Herod brought together the chief priests and the teachers of the Law of Moses and asked them, "Where will the Messiah be born?"

[5]They told him, "He will be born in Bethlehem, just as the prophet wrote.

[9]The wise men listened to what the king said and then left. And the star they had seen in the east went on ahead of them until it stopped over the place where the child was. [10]They were thrilled and excited to see the star.

[11]When the men went into the house and saw the child with Mary, his mother, they knelt down and worshiped him. They took out their gifts of gold, frankincense, and myrrh[c] and gave them to him. [12]Later they were warned in a dream not to return to Herod, and they went back home by another road.

[a]2.1 *wise men:* People famous for studying the stars. [b]2.2 *his star in the east:* Or "his star rise."
[c]2.11 *frankincense, and myrrh:* Frankincense was a valuable powder that was burned to make a sweet smell. Myrrh was a valuable sweet-smelling powder often used in perfume.

Prayer Starter: Thank you, God, for Jesus, born on Christmas Day.

Memory Verse: Then after her baby . . .   —*Matthew 1.21*

Hiding in Egypt

After the wise men had gone, an angel from the Lord appeared to Joseph in a dream and said, "Get up! Hurry and take the child and his mother to Egypt! Stay there until I tell you to return, because Herod is looking for the child and wants to kill him."

¹⁴That night, Joseph got up and took his wife and the child to Egypt, ¹⁵where they stayed until Herod died. So the Lord's promise came true, just as the prophet had said, "I called my son out of Egypt."

¹⁶When Herod found out that the wise men from the east had tricked him, he was very angry. He gave orders for his men to kill all the boys who lived in or near Bethlehem and were two years old and younger. This was based on what he had learned from the wise men.

¹⁷So the Lord's promise came true, just as the prophet Jeremiah had said,

[18] "In Ramah a voice was heard
    crying and weeping loudly.
Rachel was mourning for her children,
and she refused to be comforted,
    because they were dead."

[19]After King Herod died, an angel from the Lord appeared in a dream to Joseph while he was still in Egypt. [20]The angel said, "Get up and take the child and his mother back to Israel. The people who wanted to kill him are now dead."

[21]Joseph got up and left with them for Israel. [22]But when he heard that Herod's son Archelaus was now ruler of Judea, he was afraid to go there. Then in a dream he was told to go to Galilee, [23]and they went to live there in the town of Nazareth. So the Lord's promise came true, just as the prophet had said, "He will be called a Nazarene."[a]

[a]2.23 *He will be called a Nazarene:* The prophet who said this is not known.

Prayer Starter: Lord, help the people of Israel and Egypt and all the other nations to know and love Jesus Christ.

Memory Verse: Then after her baby is born . . .   —*Matthew 1.21*

<table>
<tr><td>

**Jesus Is
Tested
by Satan**

</td><td>

The Holy Spirit led Jesus into the desert, so that the devil could test him. [2]After Jesus had gone without eating[a] for forty days and nights, he was very hungry. [3]Then the devil came to him and said, "If you are God's Son, tell these stones to turn into bread."

</td></tr>
</table>

[4]Jesus answered, "The Scriptures say:

'No one can live only on food.
  People need every word that God has spoken.'"

[5]Next, the devil took Jesus to the holy city and had him stand on the highest part of the temple. [6]The devil said, "If you are God's son, jump off. The Scriptures say:

'God will give his angels orders about you.
They will catch you in their arms,
    and you won't hurt your feet on the stones.'"

[7]Jesus answered, "The Scriptures also say, 'Don't try to test the Lord your God!'"

[8]Finally, the devil took Jesus up on a very high mountain and showed him all the kingdoms on earth and their power. [9]The devil said to him, "I will give all this to you, if you will bow down and worship me."

[10]Jesus answered, "Go away Satan! The Scriptures say:

'Worship the Lord your God
    and serve only him.'"

[11]Then the devil left Jesus, and angels came to help him.

[a]4.2 *went without eating:* The Jewish people sometimes went without eating (also called "fasting") to show their love for God or to show sorrow for their sins.

Prayer Starter: Keep us safe from the devil's traps, Lord. Deliver us from evil.

Memory Verse: Then after her baby is born, name him Jesus . . .
—*Matthew 1.21*

The Sermon on the Mount

Large crowds followed Jesus from Galilee and the region around the ten cities known as Decapolis.[a] They also came from Jerusalem, Judea, and from across the Jordan River.

5 When Jesus saw the crowds, he went up on the side of a mountain and sat down.[b]

Jesus' disciples gathered around him, [2]and he taught them:

[3] God blesses those people who depend only on him.
  They belong to the kingdom of heaven![c]
[4] God blesses those people who grieve.
  They will find comfort!
[5] God blesses those people who are humble.
  The earth will belong to them!
[6] God blesses those people who want to obey him[d]
more than to eat or drink.
  They will be given what they want!
[7] God blesses those people who are merciful.
  They will be treated with mercy!
[8] God blesses those people whose hearts are pure.
  They will see him!
[9] God blesses those people
who make peace.
  They will be called
  his children!
[10] God blesses those people
who are treated badly for doing right.
  They belong to the kingdom of heaven.[e]

[11]God will bless you when people insult you, mistreat you, and tell all kinds of evil lies about you because of me. [12]Be happy and excited! You will have a great reward in heaven. People did these same things to the prophets who lived long ago.

[a]4.25 *the ten cities known as Decapolis:* A group of ten cities east of Samaria and Galilee, where the people followed the Greek way of life. [b]5.1 *sat down:* Teachers in the ancient world, including Jewish teachers, usually sat down when they taught. [c]5.3 *They belong to the kingdom of heaven:* Or "The kingdom of heaven belongs to them." [d]5.6 *who want to obey him:* Or "who want to do right" or "who want everyone to be treated right." [e]5.10 *They belong to the kingdom of heaven:* Or "The kingdom of heaven belongs to them."

Prayer Starter: Lord, bless us. May we depend only on you.

Memory Verse: Then after her baby is born, name him Jesus, because he will save his people . . .
—*Matthew 1.21*

When You Pray

When you pray, don't be like those show-offs who love to stand up and pray in the meeting places and on the street corners. They do this just to look good. I can assure you that they already have their reward.

⁶When you pray, go into a room alone and close the door. Pray to your Father in private. He knows what is done in private, and he will reward you.

⁷When you pray, don't talk on and on as people do who don't know God. They think God likes to hear long prayers. ⁸Don't be like them. Your Father knows what you need before you ask.

⁹You should pray like this:

> Our Father in heaven
> help us to honor your name.
> ¹⁰ Come and set up your kingdom,
> so that everyone on earth
> will obey you,
>   as you are obeyed in heaven.
> ¹¹ Give us our food for today.ᵃ
> ¹² Forgive us for doing wrong,
>   as we forgive others.
> ¹³ Keep us from being tempted
>   and protect us from evil.ᵇ

¹⁴If you forgive others for the wrongs they do to you, your Father in heaven will forgive you. ¹⁵But if you don't forgive others, your Father will not forgive your sins.

¹⁶When you go without eating,ᶜ don't try to look gloomy as those show-offs do when they go without eating. I can assure you that they already have their reward. ¹⁷Instead, comb your hair and wash your face. ¹⁸Then others won't know that you are going without eating. But your Father sees what is done in private, and he will reward you.

ᵃ6.11 *our food for today:* Or "the food that we need" or "our food for the coming day." ᵇ6.13 *evil:* Or "the evil one," that is, the devil. Some manuscripts add, "the kingdom, the power, and the glory are yours forever. Amen." ᶜ6.16 *without eating:* The Jewish people sometimes went without eating (also called "fasting") to show their love for God or to show sorrow for their sins.

Prayer Starter: Our Father in heaven, help us to honor your name.

Memory Verse: Then after her baby is born, name him Jesus, because he will save his people from their sins.   *—Matthew 1.21*

Don't Worry

You cannot be the slave of two masters! You will like one more than the other or be more loyal to one than the other. You cannot serve both God and money.

²⁵I tell you not to worry about your life. Don't worry about having something to eat, drink, or wear. Isn't life more than food or clothing? ²⁶Look at the birds in the sky! They don't plant or harvest. They don't even store grain in barns. Yet your Father in heaven takes care of them. Aren't you worth more than birds?

²⁷Can worry make you live longer?ᵃ ²⁸Why worry about clothes? Look how the wild flowers grow. They don't work hard to make their clothes. ²⁹But I tell you that Solomon with all his wealthᵇ wasn't as well clothed as one of them. ³⁰God gives such beauty to everything that grows in the fields, even though it is here today and thrown into a fire tomorrow. He will surely do even more for you! Why do you have such little faith?

³¹Don't worry and ask yourselves, "Will we have anything to eat? Will we have anything to drink? Will we have any clothes to wear?" ³²Only people who don't know God are always worrying about such things. Your Father in heaven knows that you need all of these. ³³But more than anything else, put God's work first and do what he wants. Then the other things will be yours as well.

ᵃ6.27 *live longer:* Or "grow taller." ᵇ6.29 *Solomon with all his wealth:* The Jewish people thought that Solomon was the richest person who had ever lived.

Prayer Starter: Keep me from worry, dear Lord, for I know you love and care for me.

Memory Verse: But more than anything else . . .   —*Matthew 6.33*

Jesus Walks on Water

Right away, Jesus made his disciples get into a boat and start back across the lake.[a] But he stayed until he had sent the crowds away. ²³Then he went up on a mountain where he could be alone and pray. Later that evening, he was still there.

²⁴By this time the boat was a long way from the shore. It was going against the wind and was being tossed around by the waves. ²⁵A little while before morning, Jesus came walking on the water toward his disciples. ²⁶When they saw him, they thought he was a ghost. They were terrified and started screaming.

²⁷At once, Jesus said to them, "Don't worry! I am Jesus. Don't be afraid."

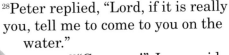

²⁸Peter replied, "Lord, if it is really you, tell me to come to you on the water."

²⁹"Come on!" Jesus said. Peter then got out of the boat and started walking on the water toward him.

³⁰But when Peter saw how strong the wind was, he was afraid and started sinking, "Save me, Lord!" he shouted.

³¹Right away, Jesus reached out his hand. He helped Peter up and said, "You surely don't have much faith. Why do you doubt?"

³²When Jesus and Peter got into the boat, the wind died down. ³³The men in the boat worshiped Jesus and said, "You really are the Son of God!"

³⁴Jesus and his disciples crossed the lake and came to shore near the town of Gennesaret. ³⁵The people found out that he was there, and they sent word to everyone who lived in that part of the country. So they brought all the sick people to Jesus. ³⁶They begged him just to let them touch his clothes, and everyone who did was healed.

[a]14.22 *back across the lake:* To the west side.

Prayer Starter: Give me a stronger faith, dear Lord.

Memory Verse: But more than anything else, put God's work first . . .
—*Matthew 6.33*

Jesus Is the Messiah

When Jesus and his disciples were near the town of Caesarea Philippi, he asked them, "What do people say about the Son of Man?"

[14]The disciples answered, "Some people say you are John the Baptist or maybe Elijah[a] or Jeremiah or some other prophet."

[15]Then Jesus asked them, "But who do you say I am?"

[16]Simon Peter spoke up, "You are the Messiah, the Son of the living God."

[17]Jesus told him:

Simon, son of Jonah, you are blessed! You didn't discover this on your own. It was shown to you by my Father in heaven. [18]So I will call you Peter, which means "a rock." On this rock I will build my church, and death itself will not have any power over it. [19]I will give you the keys to the kingdom of heaven, and God in heaven will allow whatever you allow on earth. But he will not allow anything that you don't allow.

[20]Jesus told his disciples not to tell anyone that he was the Messiah.

[21]From then on, Jesus began telling his disciples what would happen to him. He said, "I must go to Jerusalem. There the nation's leaders, the chief priests, and the teachers of the Law of Moses will make me suffer terribly. I will be killed, but three days later I will rise to life."

[24]Then Jesus said to his disciples:

If any of you want to be my followers, you must forget about yourself. You must take up your cross and follow me.

[a]16.14 *Elijah:* Many of the Jewish people expected the prophet Elijah to come and prepare the way for the Messiah.

Prayer Starter: I praise you, O God, for Jesus, the Messiah, Son of the living God.

Memory Verse: But more than anything else, put God's work first and do what he wants . . .
—*Matthew 6.33*

Jesus, Moses, and Elijah

Six days later Jesus took Peter and the brothers James and John with him. They went up on a very high mountain where they could be alone. [2]There in front of the disciples, Jesus was completely changed. His face was shining like the sun, and his clothes became white as light.

[3]All at once Moses and Elijah were there talking with Jesus. [4]So Peter said to him, "Lord, it is good for us to be here! Let us make three shelters, one for you, one for Moses, and one for Elijah."

[5]While Peter was still speaking, the shadow of a bright cloud passed over them. From the cloud a voice said, "This is my own dear Son, and I am pleased with him. Listen to what he says!" [6]When the disciples heard the voice, they were so afraid that they fell flat on the ground. [7]But Jesus came over and touched them. He said, "Get up and don't be afraid!" [8]When they opened their eyes, they saw only Jesus.

[9]On their way down from the mountain, Jesus warned his disciples not to tell anyone what they had seen until after the Son of Man had been raised from death.

[10]The disciples asked Jesus, "Don't the teachers of the Law of Moses say that Elijah must come before the Messiah does?"

[11]Jesus told them, "Elijah certainly will come and get everything ready. [12]In fact, he has already come. But the people did not recognize him and treated him just as they wanted to. They will soon make the Son of Man suffer in the same way." [13]Then the disciples understood that Jesus was talking to them about John the Baptist.

Prayer Starter: I love your Word, Lord. Thank you for every verse in the Bible.

Memory Verse: But more than anything else, put God's work first and do what he wants. Then the other things . . . —*Matthew 6.33*

Jesus Enters Jerusalem

When Jesus and his disciples came near Jerusalem, he went to Bethphage on the Mount of Olives and sent two of them on ahead. ²He told them, "Go into the next village, where you will at once find a donkey and her colt. Untie the two donkeys and bring them to me. ³If anyone asks why you are doing that, just say, 'The Lord[a] needs them.' Right away he will let you have the donkeys."

⁴So God's promise came true, just as the prophet had said,

⁵ "Announce to the people of Jerusalem:
  'Your king is coming to you!
He is humble and rides on a donkey.
  He comes on the colt of a donkey.'"

⁶The disciples left and did what Jesus had told them to do. ⁷They brought the donkey and its colt and laid some clothes on their backs. Then Jesus got on.

⁸Many people spread clothes in the road, while others put down branches[b] which they had cut from trees. ⁹Some people walked ahead of Jesus and others followed behind. They were all shouting,

"Hooray[c] for the Son of David![d]
God bless the one who comes in the name of the Lord.
  Hooray for God in heaven above!"

¹⁰When Jesus came to Jerusalem, everyone in the city was excited and asked, "Who can this be?"

¹¹The crowd answered, "This is Jesus, the prophet from Nazareth in Galilee."

[a]21.3 *The Lord:* Or "The master of the donkeys." [b]21.8 *spread clothes . . . put down branches:* This was one way that the Jewish people welcomed a famous person. [c]21.9 *Hooray:* This translates a word that can mean "please save us." But it is most often used as a shout of praise to God. [d]21.9 *Son of David:* The Jewish people expected the Messiah to be from the family of King David, and for this reason the Messiah was often called the "Son of David."

Prayer Starter: Hooray for the Son of David! Hooray for Jesus!

Memory Verse: But more than anything else, put God's work first and do what he wants. Then the other things will be yours as well.
—*Matthew 6.33*

Peter Denies Jesus

After Jesus had been arrested, he was led off to the house of Caiaphas the high priest. The nation's leaders and the teachers of the Law of Moses were meeting there. 58But Peter followed along at a distance and came to the courtyard of the high priest's palace. He went in and sat down with the guards to see what was going to happen.

59The chief priests and the whole council wanted to put Jesus to death. So they tried to find some people who would tell lies about him in court.[a]

69While Peter was sitting out in the courtyard, a servant girl came up to him and said, "You were with Jesus from Galilee."

70But in front of everyone Peter said, "That isn't so! I don't know what you are talking about!"

71When Peter had gone out to the gate, another servant girl saw him and said to some people there, "This man was with Jesus from Nazareth."

72Again Peter denied it, and this time he swore, "I don't even know that man!"

73A little while later some people standing there walked over to Peter and said, "We know that you are one of them. We can tell it because you talk like someone from Galilee."

74Peter began to curse and swear, "I don't know that man!"

Right then a rooster crowed.

[a]26.59 *some people who would tell lies about him in court:* The Law of Moses taught that two witnesses were necessary before a person could be put to death.

Prayer Starter: Dear God, keep me from ever being ashamed of being a Christian.

Memory Verse: Jesus healed . . .   —*Mark 1.34*

Pilate the Governor

During Passover the governor always freed a prisoner chosen by the people. [16]At that time a well-known terrorist named Jesus Barabbas[a] was in jail. [17]So when the crowd came together, Pilate asked them, "Which prisoner do you want me to set free? Do you want Jesus Barabbas or Jesus who is called the Messiah?" [18]Pilate knew that the leaders had brought Jesus to him because they were jealous.

[19]While Pilate was judging the case, his wife sent him a message. It said, "Don't have anything to do with that innocent man. I have had nightmares because of him."

[20]But the chief priests and the leaders convinced the crowds to ask for Barabbas to be set free and for Jesus to be killed. [21]Pilate asked the crowd again, "Which of these two men do you want me to set free?"

"Barabbas!" they replied.

[22]Pilate asked them, "What am I to do with Jesus, who is called the Messiah?"

They all yelled, "Nail him to a cross!"

[23]Pilate answered, "But what crime has he done?"

"Nail him to a cross!" they yelled even louder.

[24]Pilate saw that there was nothing he could do and that the people were starting to riot. So he took some water and washed his hands[b] in front of them and said, "I won't have anything to do with killing this man. You are the ones doing it!"

[25]Everyone answered, "We and our descendants will take the blame for his death!"

[26]Pilate set Barabbas free. Then he ordered his soldiers to beat Jesus with a whip and nail him to a cross.

[a]27.16 *Jesus Barabbas:* Here and in verse 17 many manuscripts have "Barabbas." [b]27.24 *washed his hands:* To show that he was innocent.

Prayer Starter: How can I ever thank you enough for the Lord Jesus Christ?

Memory Verse: Jesus healed all kinds of terrible diseases . . .
—*Mark 1.34*

Jesus Heals the Sick

Everyone was amazed at his teaching. He taught with authority, and not like the teachers of the Law of Moses. ²³Suddenly a man with an evil spirit[a] in him entered the meeting place and yelled. ²⁴"Jesus from Nazareth, what do you want with us? Have you come to destroy us? I know who you are! You are God's Holy One."

²⁵Jesus told the evil spirit, "Be quiet and come out of the man!" ²⁶The spirit shook him. Then it gave a loud shout and left.

²⁷Everyone was completely surprised and kept saying to each other, "What is this? It must be some new kind of powerful teaching! Even the evil spirits obey him." ²⁸News about Jesus quickly spread all over Galilee.

²⁹As soon as Jesus left the meeting place with James and John, they went home with Simon and Andrew. ³⁰When they got there, Jesus was told that Simon's mother-in-law was sick in bed with fever. ³¹Jesus went to her. He took hold of her hand and helped her up. The fever left her, and she served them a meal.

³²That evening after sunset,[b] all who were sick or had demons in them were brought to Jesus. ³³In fact, the whole town gathered around the door of the house. ³⁴Jesus healed all kinds of terrible diseases and forced out a lot of demons. But the demons knew who he was, and he did not let them speak.

[a]1.23 *evil spirit:* A Jewish person who had an evil spirit was considered "unclean" and was not allowed to eat or worship with other Jewish people. [b]1.32 *after sunset:* The Sabbath was over, and a new day began at sunset.

Prayer Starter: Dear God, help me to tell the good news about Jesus to someone this week.

Memory Verse: Jesus healed all kinds of terrible diseases and forced out a lot of demons . . .
      —*Mark 1.34*

Lots of Evil Spirits

Jesus and his disciples crossed Lake Galilee and came to shore near the town of Gerasa.[a] [2]When he was getting out of the boat, a man with an evil spirit quickly ran to him [3]from the graveyard[b] where he had been living. No one was able to tie the man up anymore, not even with a chain. [4]He had often been put in chains and leg irons, but he broke the chains and smashed the leg irons. No one could control him. [5]Night and day he was in the graveyard or on the hills, yelling and cutting himself with stones.

[6]When the man saw Jesus in the distance, he ran up to him and knelt down. [7]He shouted, "Jesus, Son of God in heaven, what do you want with me? Promise me in God's name that you won't torture me!" [8]The man said this because Jesus had already told the evil spirit to come out of him.

[9]Jesus asked, "What is your name?"

The man answered, "My name is Lots, because I have 'lots' of evil spirits." [10]He then begged Jesus not to send them away.

[11]Over on the hillside a large herd of pigs was feeding. [12]So the evil spirits begged Jesus, "Send us into those pigs! Let us go into them." [13]Jesus let them go, and they went out of the man and into the pigs. The whole herd of about two thousand pigs rushed down the steep bank into the lake and drowned.

[a]5.1 *Gerasa:* Some manuscripts have "Gadara," and others have "Gergesa." [b]5.3 *graveyard:* It was thought that demons and evil spirits lived in graveyards.

Prayer Starter: You are stonger than the devil and all the demons, God. You are Lord over all the earth.

Memory Verse: Jesus healed all kinds of terrible diseases and forced out a lot of demons. But the demons knew who he was . . .
—*Mark 1.34*

Jairus

Once again Jesus got into the boat and crossed Lake Galilee.[a] Then as he stood on the shore, a large crowd gathered around him. [22]The person in charge of the Jewish meeting place was also there. His name was Jairus, and when he saw Jesus, he went over to him. He knelt at Jesus' feet [23]and started begging him for help. He said, "My daughter is about to die! Please come and touch her, so she will get well and live." [24]Jesus went with Jairus. Many people followed along and kept crowding around.

[35]While Jesus was still speaking, some men came from Jairus' home and said, "Your daughter has died! Why bother the teacher anymore?"

[36]Jesus heard[b] what they said, and he said to Jairus, "Don't worry. Just have faith!"

[37]Jesus did not let anyone go with him except Peter and the two brothers, James and John. [38]They went home with Jairus and saw the people crying and making a lot of noise.[c] [39]Then Jesus went inside and said to them, "Why are you crying and carrying on like this? The child isn't dead. She is just asleep." [40]But the people laughed at him.

After Jesus had sent them all out of the house, he took the girl's father and mother and his three disciples and went to where she was. [41-42]He took the twelve-year-old girl by the hand and said, "Talitha, koum!"[d] which means, "Little girl, get up!" The girl got right up and started walking around.

[a]5.21 *crossed Lake Galilee:* To the west side. [b]5.36 *heard:* Or "ignored." [c]5.38 *crying and making a lot of noise:* The Jewish people often hired mourners for funerals. [d]5.41,42 *Talitha, koum:* These words are in Aramaic, a language spoken in Palestine during the time of Jesus.

Prayer Starter: O God, keep me from worry. Give me faith instead of fear.

Memory Verse: Jesus healed all kinds of terrible diseases and forced out a lot of demons. But the demons knew who he was, and he did not let them speak.
                                                          —*Mark 1.34*

Jesus Feeds Five Thousand

After the apostles returned to Jesus,[a] they told him everything they had done and taught. [31]But so many people were coming and going that Jesus and the apostles did not even have a chance to eat. Then Jesus said, "Let's go to a place[b] where we can be alone and get some rest." [32]They left in a boat for a place where they could be alone. [33]But many people saw them leave and figured out where they were going. So people from every town ran on ahead and got there first.

[34]When Jesus got out of the boat, he saw the large crowd that was like sheep without a shepherd. He felt sorry for the people and started teaching them many things.

[35]That evening the disciples came to Jesus and said, "This place is like a desert, and it is already late. [36]Let the crowds leave, so they can go to the farms and villages near here and buy something to eat."

[37]Jesus replied, "You give them something to eat."

But they asked him, "Don't you know that it would take almost a year's wages[c] to buy all of these people something to eat?"

[38]Then Jesus said, "How much bread do you have? Go and see!"

They found out and answered, "We have five small loaves of bread[d] and two fish." [39]Jesus told his disciples to have the people sit down on the green grass. [40]They sat down in groups of a hundred and groups of fifty.

[41]Jesus took the five loaves and the two fish. He looked up toward heaven and blessed the food. Then be broke the bread and handed it to his disciples to give to the people. He also divided the two fish, so that everyone could have some.

[42]After everyone had eaten all they wanted, [43]Jesus' disciples picked up twelve large baskets of leftover bread and fish.

[44]There were five thousand men who ate the food.

---

[a]6.30 *the apostles returned to Jesus:* From the mission on which he had sent them. [b]6.31 *a place:* This was probably northeast of Lake Galilee. [c]6.37 *almost a year's wages:* The Greek text has "two hundred silver coins." Each coin was the average day's wage for a worker. [d]6.38 *loaves of bread:* These would have been flat and round or in the shape of a bun.

Prayer Starter: Thank you, Lord, for fish and bread and pizzas and cherry pies, and for all good things to eat.

Memory Verse: Let the children come to me! . . . —*Mark 10.14b*

Jesus Blesses Children

Some Pharisees wanted to test Jesus. So they came up to him and asked if it was right for a man to divorce his wife. ³Jesus asked them, "What does the Law of Moses say about that?"

⁴They answered, "Moses allows a man to write out divorce papers and send his wife away."

⁵Jesus replied, "Moses gave you this law because you are so heartless. ⁶But in the beginning God made a man and a woman. ⁷That's why a man leaves his father and mother and gets married. ⁸He becomes like one person with his wife. Then they are no longer two people, but one. ⁹And no one should separate a couple that God has joined together."

¹⁰When Jesus and his disciples were back in the house, they asked him about what he had said. ¹¹He told them, "A man who divorces his wife and marries someone else is unfaithful to his wife. ¹²A woman who divorces her husbandª and marries again is also unfaithful."

¹³Some people brought their children to Jesus so that he could bless them by placing his hands on them. But his disciples told the people to stop bothering him.

¹⁴When Jesus saw this, he became angry and said, "Let the children come to me! Don't try to stop them. People who are like these little children belong to the kingdom of God.ᵇ ¹⁵I promise you that you cannot get into God's kingdom, unless you accept it the way a child does." ¹⁶Then Jesus took the children in his arms and blessed them by placing his hands on them.

ª10.12 *A woman who divorces her husband:* Roman law let a woman divorce her husband, but Jewish law did not let a woman do this. ᵇ10.14 *People who are like these little children belong to the kingdom of God:* Or "The kingdom of God belongs to people who are like these little children."

Prayer Starter: Thank you, Lord, for loving me. Thank you for blessing me.

Memory Verse: Let the children come to me! Don't try to stop them. . . .   *—Mark 10.14b*

The Lord's Supper

It was the first day of the Festival of Thin Bread, and the Passover lambs were being killed. Jesus' disciples asked him, "Where do you want us to prepare the Passover meal?"

[13]Jesus said to two of the disciples, "Go into the city, where you will meet a man carrying a jar of water.[a] Follow him, [14]and when he goes into a house, say to the owner, 'Our teacher wants to know if you have room where he can eat the Passover meal with his disciples.' [15]The owner will take you upstairs and show you a large room furnished and ready for you to use. Prepare the meal there."

[16]The two disciples went into the city and found everything just as Jesus had told them. So they prepared the Passover meal.

[17-18]While Jesus and the twelve disciples were eating together that evening, he said, "The one who will betray me is now eating with me."

[19]This made the disciples sad, and one after another they said to Jesus, "You surely don't mean me!"

[20]He answered, "It is one of you twelve men who is eating from this dish with me. [21]The Son of Man will die, just as the Scriptures say. But it is going to be terrible for the one who betrays me. That man would be better off if he had never been born."

[22]During the meal Jesus took some bread in his hands. He blessed

the bread and broke it. Then he gave it to his disciples and said, "Take this. It is my body."

[23]Jesus picked up a cup of wine and gave thanks to God. He gave it to his disciples, and they all drank some. [24]Then he said, "This is my blood, which is poured out for many people, and with it God makes his agreement. [25]From now on I will not drink any wine, until I drink new wine in God's kingdom." [26]Then they sang a hymn and went out to the Mount of Olives.

[a]14.13 *a man carrying a jar of water:* A male slave carrying water could mean that the family was rich.

Prayer Starter: O God, thank you for giving us Jesus, your Son, through the Eucharist.

Memory Verse: Let the children come to me! Don't try to stop them. People who are like . . .　　*—Mark 10.14b*

Nail Jesus to a Cross

Early the next morning the chief priests, the nation's leaders, and the teachers of the Law of Moses met together with the whole Jewish council. They tied up Jesus and led him off to Pilate.

²He asked Jesus, "Are you the king of the Jews?"

"Those are your words," Jesus answered.

³The chief priests brought many charges against Jesus. ⁴Then Pilate questioned him again, "Don't you have anything to say? Don't you hear what crimes they say you have done?" ⁵But Jesus did not answer, and Pilate was amazed.

⁶During Passover, Pilate always freed one prisoner chosen by the people. ⁷And at that time there was a prisoner named Barabbas. He and some others had been arrested for murder during a riot. ⁸The crowd now came and asked Pilate to set a prisoner free, just as he usually did.

[9]Pilate asked them, "Do you want me to free the king of the Jews?" [10]Pilate knew that the chief priests had brought Jesus to him because they were jealous.

[11]But the chief priests told the crowd to ask Pilate to free Barabbas.

[12]Then Pilate asked the crowd, "What do you want me to do with this man you say is[a] the king of the Jews?"

[13]They yelled, "Nail him to a cross!"

[14]Pilate asked, "But what crime has he done?"

"Nail him to a cross!" they yelled even louder.

[15]Pilate wanted to please the crowd. So he set Barabbas free. Then he ordered his soldiers to beat Jesus with a whip and nail him to a cross.

[a]15.12 *this man you say is:* These words are not in some manuscripts.

Prayer Starter: I love you, Jesus, for suffering for me.

Memory Verse: Let the children come to me! Don't try to stop them. People who are like these little children . . .   —*Mark 10.14b*

Soldiers Make Fun of Jesus

The soldiers led Jesus inside the courtyard of the fortress[a] and called together the rest of the troops. [17]They put a purple robe[b] on him, and on his head they placed a crown that they had made out of thorn branches. [18]They made fun of Jesus and shouted, "Hey, you king of the Jews!" [19]Then they beat him on the head with a stick. They spit on him and knelt down and pretended to worship him.

[20]When the soldiers had finished making fun of Jesus, they took off the purple robe. They put his own clothes back on him and led him off to be nailed to a cross. [21]Simon from Cyrene happened to be coming in from a farm, and they forced him to carry Jesus' cross. Simon was the father of Alexander and Rufus.

[22]The soldiers took Jesus to Golgotha, which means "Place of a Skull."[c] [23]There they gave him some wine mixed with a drug to ease the pain, but he refused to drink it.

[24]They nailed Jesus to a cross and gambled to see who would get his clothes. [25]It was about nine o'clock in the morning when they nailed him to the cross.

[26]On it was a sign that told why he was nailed there. It read, "This is the King of the Jews." [27-28]The soldiers also nailed two criminals on crosses, one to the right of Jesus and the other to his left.[d]

[a]15.16 *fortress:* The place where the Roman governor stayed. It was probably at Herod's palace west of Jerusalem, though it may have been Fortress Antonia, north of the temple, where the Roman troops were stationed. [b]15.17 *purple robe:* This was probably a Roman soldier's robe. [c]15.22 *Place of a Skull:* The place was probably given this name because it was near a large rock in the shape of a human skull. [d]15.27,28 *left:* Some manuscripts add, "So the Scriptures came true which say, 'He was accused of being a criminal.'"

Prayer Starter: Thank you, Lord, thank you for Christ Jesus.

Memory Verse: Let the children come to me! Don't try to stop them. People who are like these little children belong to the kingdom of God.
—Mark 10.14b

An Angel Visits Mary

God sent the angel Gabriel to the town of Nazareth in Galilee ²⁷with a message for a virgin named Mary. She was engaged to Joseph from the family of King David. ²⁸The angel greeted Mary and said, "You are truly blessed! The Lord is with you."

²⁹Mary was confused by the angel's words and wondered what they meant. ³⁰Then the angel told Mary, "Don't be afraid! God is pleased with you, ³¹and you will have a son. His name will be Jesus. ³²He will be great and will be called the Son of God Most High. The Lord God will make him king, as his ancestor David was. ³³He will rule the people of Israel forever, and his kingdom will never end."

³⁴Mary asked the angel, "How can this happen? I am not married!"

³⁵The angel answered, "The Holy Spirit will come down to you, and God's power will come over you. So your child will be called the holy Son of God. ³⁶Your relative Elizabeth is also going to have a son, even though she is old. No one thought she could ever have a baby, but in three months she will have a son. ³⁷Nothing is impossible for God!"

³⁸Mary said, "I am the Lord's servant! Let it happen as you have said." And the angel left her.

Prayer Starter: I am your servant, Lord. Use me.

Memory Verse: Jesus became wise . . .   —*Luke 2.52*

Mary and Elizabeth

A short time later Mary hurried to a town in the hill country of Judea. ⁴⁰She went into Zechariah's home, where she greeted Elizabeth. ⁴¹When Elizabeth heard Mary's greeting, her baby moved within her.

The Holy Spirit came upon Elizabeth. ⁴²Then in a loud voice she said to Mary:

God has blessed you more than any other woman! He has also blessed the child you will have. ⁴³Why should the mother of my Lord come to me? ⁴⁴As soon as I heard your greeting, my baby became happy and moved within me. ⁴⁵The Lord has blessed you because you believed that he will keep his promise.

⁴⁶Mary said:

With all my heart ⁴⁷I praise the Lord,
and I am glad because of God my Savior.
⁴⁸ God cares for me, his humble servant.
From now on, all people will say
God has blessed me.
⁴⁹ God All-Powerful has done great things for me,
and his name is holy.
⁵⁰ He always shows mercy
to everyone who worships him.
⁵¹ The Lord has used his powerful arm
to scatter those who are proud.
⁵² God drags strong rulers from their thrones
and puts humble people in places of power.
⁵³ God gives the hungry good things to eat,
and sends the rich away
with nothing.
⁵⁴ God helps his servant Israel
and is always merciful to his people.
⁵⁵ The Lord made this promise to our ancestors,
to Abraham and his family forever!

⁵⁶Mary stayed with Elizabeth about three months. Then she went back home.

Prayer Starter: With all my heart, I praise the Lord.

Memory Verse: Jesus became wise, and he grew strong. . . .
—*Luke 2.52*

Jesus Is Born

About that time Emperor Augustus gave orders for the names of all the people to be listed in record books.[a] ²These first records were made when Quirinius was governor of Syria.[b]

³Everyone had to go to their own hometown to be listed. ⁴So Joseph had to leave Nazareth in Galilee and go to Bethlehem in Judea. Long ago Bethlehem had been King David's hometown, and Joseph went there because he was from David's family.

⁵Mary was engaged to Joseph and traveled with him to Bethlehem. She was soon going to have a baby, ⁶and while they were there, ⁷she gave birth to her first-born[c] son. She dressed him in baby clothes[d] and laid him on a bed of hay, because there was no room for them in the inn.

⁸That night in the fields near Bethlehem some shepherds were guarding their sheep. ⁹All at once an angel came down to them from the Lord, and the brightness of the Lord's glory flashed around them. The shepherds were frightened. ¹⁰But the angel said, "Don't be afraid! I have good news for you, which will make everyone happy. ¹¹This very day in King David's hometown a Savior was born for you. He is Christ the Lord. ¹²You will know who he is, because you will find him dressed in baby clothes and lying on a bed of hay."

¹³Suddenly many other angels came down from heaven and joined in praising God. They said:

¹⁴"Praise God in heaven!
Peace on earth to everyone
who pleases God."

¹⁵After the angels had left and gone back to heaven, the shepherds said to each other, "Let's go to Bethlehem and see what the Lord has told us about." ¹⁶They hurried off and found Mary and Joseph, and they saw the baby lying on a bed of hay.

---

[a]2.1 *names . . . listed in record books:* This was done so that everyone could be made to pay taxes to the Emperor. [b]2.2 *Quirinius was governor of Syria:* It is known that Quirinius made a record of the people in A.D. 6 or 7. But the exact date of the record taking that Luke mentions is not known. [c]2.7 *first-born:* The Jewish people said that the first-born son in each of their families belonged to the Lord. [d]2.7 *dressed him in baby clothes:* The Greek text has "wrapped him in wide strips of cloth," which was how young babies were dressed.

Prayer Starter: Thank you, Lord, for sending Jesus. Help me to think about him this Christmas.

Memory Verse: Jesus became wise, and he grew strong. God was pleased . . .

—Luke 2.52

Simeon and Anna

At this time a man named Simeon was living in Jerusalem. Simeon was a good man. He loved God and was waiting for God to save the people of Israel. God's Spirit came to him [26]and told him that he would not die until he had seen Christ the Lord.

[27]When Mary and Joseph brought Jesus to the temple to do what the Law of Moses says should be done for a new baby, the Spirit told Simeon to go into the temple. [28]Simeon took the baby Jesus in his arms and praised God,

[29] "Lord, I am your servant,
and now I can die in peace,
because you have kept your promise to me.
[30] With my own eyes I have seen
what you have done to save your people,
[31] and foreign nations will also see this.
[32] Your mighty power is a light for all nations,
and it will bring honor to your people Israel."

[33]Jesus' parents were surprised at what Simeon had said. [34]Then he blessed them and told Mary, "This child of yours will cause many people in Israel to fall and others to stand. The child will be like a warning sign. Many people will reject him, [35]and you, Mary, will suffer as though you had been stabbed by a dagger. But all this will show what people are really thinking."

[36]The prophet Anna was also there in the temple. She was the daughter of Phanuel from the tribe of Asher, and she was very old. In her youth she had been married for seven years, but her husband died. [37]And now she was eighty-four years old.[a] Night and day she served God in the temple by praying and often going without eating.[b]

³⁸At that time Anna came in and praised God. She spoke about the child Jesus to everyone who hoped for Jerusalem to be set free.

^a2.37 *And now she was eighty-four years old:* Or "And now she had been a widow for eighty-four years." ^b2.37 *without eating:* The Jewish people sometimes went without eating (also called "fasting") to show their love for God or to show sorrow for their sins.

Prayer Starter: Lord, your mighty power is a light for all the nations.

Memory Verse: Jesus became wise, and he grew strong. God was pleased with him . . .
—*Luke 2.52*

The Child Jesus Is Lost

After Joseph and Mary had done everything that the Law of the Lord commands, they returned home to Nazareth in Galilee. ⁴⁰The child Jesus grew. He became strong and wise, and God blessed him.

⁴¹Every year Jesus' parents went to Jerusalem for Passover. ⁴²And when Jesus was twelve years old, they all went there as usual for the celebration. ⁴³After Passover his parents left, but they did not know that Jesus had stayed on in the city. ⁴⁴They thought he was traveling with some other people, and they went a whole day before they started looking for him. ⁴⁵When they could not find him with their relatives and friends, they went back to Jerusalem and started looking for him there.

⁴⁶Three days later they found Jesus sitting in the temple, listening to the teachers and asking them questions. ⁴⁷Everyone who heard him was surprised at how much he knew and at the answers he gave.

⁴⁸When his parents found him, they were amazed. His mother said, "Son, why have you done this to us? Your father and I have been very worried, and we have been searching for you!"

⁴⁹Jesus answered, "Why did you have to look for me? Didn't you know that I would be in my Father's house?"ᵃ ⁵⁰But they did not understand what he meant.

⁵¹Jesus went back to Nazareth with his parents and obeyed them. His mother kept on thinking about all that had happened.

⁵²Jesus became wise, and he grew strong. God was pleased with him and so were the people.

ᵃ2.49 *in my Father's house:* Or "doing my Father's work."

Prayer Starter: May I be like Jesus, dear Father. Make me wise and strong.

Memory Verse: Jesus became wise, and he grew strong. God was pleased with him and so were the people.   —*Luke 2.52*

John the Baptist

For fifteen years[a] Emperor Tiberius had ruled that part of the world. Pontius Pilate was governor of Judea, and Herod[b] was the ruler of Galilee. Herod's brother, Philip, was the ruler in the countries of Iturea and Trachonitis, and Lysanias was the ruler of Abilene. [2]Annas and Caiaphas were the Jewish high priests.[c]

At that time God spoke to Zechariah's son John, who was living in the desert. [3]So John went along the Jordan Valley, telling the people, "Turn back to God and be baptized! Then your sins will be forgiven." [4]Isaiah the prophet wrote about John when he said,

> "In the desert someone is shouting,
> 'Get the road ready for the Lord!
>   Make a straight path for him.
> [5] Fill up every valley and level every mountain and hill.
> Straighten the crooked paths
>   and smooth out the rough roads.
> [6] Then everyone will see the saving power of God.'"

[15]Everyone became excited and wondered, "Could John be the Messiah?"

[16]John said, "I am just baptizing with water. But someone more powerful is going to come, and I am not good enough even to untie his sandals.[d] He will baptize you with the Holy Spirit and with fire.

[21]While everyone else was being baptized, Jesus himself was baptized. Then as he prayed, the sky opened up, [22]and the Holy Spirit came down upon him in the form of a dove. A voice from heaven said, "You are my own dear Son, and I am pleased with you."

[a]3.1 *For fifteen years:* This was either A.D. 28 or 29, and Jesus was about thirty years old. [b]3.1 *Herod:* Herod Antipas, the son of Herod the Great. [c]3.2 *Annas and Caiaphas . . . high priests:* Annas was high priest from A.D. 6 until 15. His son-in-law Caiaphas was high priest from A.D. 18 until 37. [d]3.16 *untie his sandals:* This was the duty of a slave.

Prayer Starter: Lord, you are well pleased with your son Jesus. Be pleased with me, too.

Memory Verse: God . . .   —*Luke 7.23*

Jesus Heals a Servant

Jesus and his apostles went down from the mountain and came to some flat, level ground. Many other disciples were there to meet him. Large crowds of people from all over Judea, Jerusalem, and the coastal cities of Tyre and Sidon were there too. ¹⁸These people had come to listen to Jesus and to be healed of their diseases.

7After Jesus had finished teaching the people, he went to Capernaum. ²In that town an army officer's servant was sick and about to die. The officer liked this servant very much. ³And when he heard about Jesus, he sent some Jewish leaders to ask him to come and heal the servant.

⁴The leaders went to Jesus and begged him to do something. They said, "This man deserves your help! ⁵He loves our nation and even built us a meeting place." ⁶So Jesus went with them.

When Jesus wasn't far from the house, the officer sent some friends to tell him, "Lord, don't go to any trouble for me! I am not good enough for you to come into my house. ⁷And I am certainly not worthy to come to you. Just say the word, and my servant will get well. ⁸I have officers who give orders to me, and I have soldiers who take orders from me. I can say to one of them, 'Go!' and he goes. I can say to another, 'Come!' and he comes. I can say to my servant, 'Do this!' and he will do it."

⁹When Jesus heard this, he was so surprised that he turned and said to the crowd following him, "In all of Israel I've never found anyone with this much faith!"

¹⁰The officer's friends returned and found the servant well.

Prayer Starter: Give me faith like the officer in this story, O God.

Memory Verse: God will bless . . .   —*Luke 7.23*

Young Man, Get Up

Soon Jesus and his disciples were on their way to the town of Nain, and a big crowd was going along with them. [12]As they came near the gate of the town, they saw people carrying out the body of a widow's only son. Many people from the town were walking along with her.

[13]When the Lord saw the woman, he felt sorry for her and said, "Don't cry!"

[14]Jesus went over and touched the stretcher on which the people were carrying the dead boy. They stopped, and Jesus said, "Young man, get up!" [15]The boy sat up and began to speak. Jesus then gave him back to his mother.

[16]Everyone was frightened and praised God. They said, "A great prophet is here with us! God has come to his people."

[17]News about Jesus spread all over Judea and everywhere else in that part of the country.

[18-19]John's followers told John everything that was being said about Jesus. So he sent two of them to ask the Lord, "Are you the one we should be looking for? Or must we wait for someone else?"

[21]At that time Jesus was healing many people who were sick or in pain or were troubled by evil spirits, and he was giving sight to a lot of blind people. [22]Jesus said to the messengers sent by John, "Go and tell John what you have seen and heard. Blind people are now able to see, and the lame can walk. People who have leprosy[a] are being healed, and the deaf can now hear. The dead are raised to life, and the poor are hearing the good news. [23]God will bless everyone who doesn't reject me because of what I do."

[a]7.22 *leprosy:* In biblical times the word "leprosy" was used for many different kinds of skin diseases.

Prayer Starter: Thank you, Lord, for helping those with problems.

Memory Verse: God will bless everyone . . . —*Luke 7.23*

Woman
Washes
Jesus' Feet

APharisee invited Jesus to have dinner with him. So Jesus went to the Pharisee's home and got ready to eat.ᵃ

³⁷When a sinful woman in that town found out that Jesus was there, she bought an expensive bottle of perfume. ³⁸Then she came and stood behind Jesus. She cried and started washing his feet with her tears and drying them with her hair. The woman kissed his feet and poured the perfume on them.

³⁹The Pharisee who had invited Jesus saw this and said to himself, "If this man really were a prophet, he would know what kind of woman is touching him! He would know that she is a sinner."

⁴⁰Jesus said to the Pharisee, "Simon, I have something to say to you."

"Teacher, what is it?" Simon replied.

⁴¹Jesus told him, "Two people were in debt to a moneylender. One of them owed him five hundred silver coins, and the other owed him fifty. ⁴²Since neither of them could pay him back, the moneylender said that they didn't have to pay him anything. Which one of them will like him more?"

⁴³Simon answered, "I suppose it would be the one who had owed more and didn't have to pay it back."

"You are right," Jesus said.

⁴⁴He turned toward the woman and said to Simon, "Have you noticed this woman? When I came into your home, you didn't give me any water so I could wash my feet. But she has washed my feet with her tears and dried them with her hair. ⁴⁵You didn't greet me with a kiss, but from the

time I came in, she has not stopped kissing my feet. ⁴⁶You didn't even pour olive oil on my head,ᵇ but she has poured expensive perfume on my feet. ⁴⁷So I tell you that all her sins are forgiven, and that is why she has shown great love. But anyone who has been forgiven only a little will show only a little love."

⁴⁸Then Jesus said to the woman, "Your sins are forgiven."

⁴⁹Some other guests started saying to one another, "Who is this who dares to forgive sins?"

⁵⁰But Jesus told the woman, "Because of your faith, you are now saved.ᶜ May God give you peace!"

ᵃ7.36 *got ready to eat:* On special occasions the Jewish people often followed the Greek and Roman custom of lying down on their left side and leaning on their left elbow, while eating with their right hand. This is how the woman could come up behind Jesus and wash his feet. ᵇ7.44-46 *washed my feet . . . greet me with a kiss . . . pour olive oil on my head:* Guests in a home were usually offered water so they could wash their feet, because most people either went barefoot or wore sandals and would come in the house with very dusty feet. Guests were also greeted with a kiss on the cheek, and special ones often had sweet-smelling olive oil poured on their head. ᶜ7.50 *saved:* Or "healed." The Greek word may have either meaning.

Prayer Starter: Thank you, Lord, that you forgive my sins—no matter how big, no matter how small.

Memory Verse: God will bless everyone who doesn't reject me . . .
—Luke 7.23

The Good Samaritan

An expert in the Law of Moses stood up and asked Jesus a question to see what he would say. "Teacher," he asked, "what must I do to have eternal life?"

26Jesus answered, "What is written in the Scriptures? How do you understand them?"

27The man replied, "The Scriptures say, 'Love the Lord your God with all your heart, soul, strength, and mind.' They also say, 'Love your neighbors as much as you love yourself.'"

28Jesus said, "You have given the right answer. If you do this, you will have eternal life."

29But the man wanted to show that he knew what he was talking about. So he asked Jesus, "Who are my neighbors?"

30Jesus replied:

As a man was going down from Jerusalem to Jericho, robbers attacked him and grabbed everything he had. They beat him up and ran off, leaving him half dead. 31A priest happened to be going down the same road. But when he saw the man, he walked by on the other side. 32Later a temple helper[a] came to the same place. But when he saw the man who had been beaten up, he also went by on the other side.

33A man from Samaria then came traveling along that road. When he saw the man, he felt sorry for him 34and went over to him. He treated his wounds with olive oil and wine[b] and bandaged them. Then he put him on his own donkey and took him to an inn, where he took care of him. 35The next morning he gave the innkeeper two silver coins and said, "Please take care of the man. If you spend more than this on him, I will pay you when I return."

36Then Jesus asked, "Which one of these three people was a real neighbor to the man who was beaten up by robbers?

37The teacher answered, "The one who showed pity."

Jesus said, "Go and do the same!"

[a]10.32 *temple helper:* A man from the tribe of Levi, whose job it was to work around the temple.
[b]10.34 *olive oil and wine:* In New Testament times these were used as medicine. Sometimes olive oil is a symbol for healing by means of a miracle.

Prayer Starter: Show me someone I can help this week, Lord.

Memory Verse: God will bless everyone who doesn't reject me because of what I do.   —*Luke 7.23*

A Rich Fool

A man in a crowd said to Jesus, "Teacher, tell my brother to give me my share of what our father left us when he died."

[14]Jesus answered, "Who gave me the right to settle arguments between you and your brother?"

[15]Then he said to the crowd, "Don't be greedy! Owning a lot of things won't make your life safe."

[16]So Jesus told them this story:

A rich man's farm produced a big crop, [17]and he said to himself, "What can I do? I don't have a place large enough to store everything."

[18]Later, he said, "Now I know what I'll do. I'll tear down my barns and build bigger ones, where I can store all my grain and other goods. [19]Then I'll say to myself, 'You have stored up enough good things to last for years to come. Live it up! Eat, drink, and enjoy yourself.'"

[20]But God said to him, "You fool! Tonight you will die. Then who will get what you have stored up?"

[21]"This is what happens to people who store up everything for themselves, but are poor in the sight of God."

Prayer Starter: Thank you for taking care of all the birds, Lord, and for taking care of me.

Memory Verse: Look at the crows! . . . —*Luke 12.24*

Healing on the Sabbath

One Sabbath, Jesus was teaching in a Jewish meeting place, [11]and a woman was there who had been crippled by an evil spirit for eighteen years. She was completely bent over and could not straighten up. [12]When Jesus saw the woman, he called her over and said, "You are now well." [13]He placed his hands on her, and right away she stood up straight and praised God.

[14]The man in charge of the meeting place was angry because Jesus had healed someone on the Sabbath. So he said to the people, "Each week has six days when we can work. Come and be healed on one of those days, but not on the Sabbath."

[15]The Lord replied, "Are you trying to fool someone? Won't any one of you untie your ox or donkey and lead it out to drink on a Sabbath? [16]This woman belongs to the family of Abraham, but Satan has kept her bound for eighteen years. Isn't it right to set her free on the Sabbath?" [17]Jesus' words made his enemies ashamed. But everyone else in the crowd was happy about the wonderful things he was doing.

[18]Jesus said, "What is God's kingdom like? What can I compare it

with? ¹⁹It is like what happens when someone plants a mustard seed in a garden. The seed grows as big as a tree, and birds nest in its branches."

²⁰Then Jesus said, "What can I compare God's kingdom with? ²¹It is like what happens when a woman mixes yeast into three batches of flour. Finally, all the dough rises."

Prayer Starter: Lord, please help those who are sick today.

Memory Verse: Look at the crows! They don't plant or harvest . . .
—*Luke 12.24*

Jesus Tells Stories

Tax collectors[a] and sinners were all crowding around to listen to Jesus. [2]So the Pharisees and the teachers of the Law of Moses started grumbling, "This man is friendly with sinners. He even eats with them."

[3]Then Jesus told them this story:

[4]"If any of you has a hundred sheep, and one of them gets lost, what will you do? Won't you leave the ninety-nine in the field and go look for the lost sheep until you find it? [5]And when you find it, you will be so glad that you will put it on your shoulder [6]and carry it home. Then you will call in your friends and neighbors and say, "Let's celebrate! I've found my lost sheep."

[7]Jesus said, "In the same way there is more happiness in heaven because of one sinner who turns to God than over ninety-nine good people who don't need to."

[8]Jesus told the people another story:

What will a woman do if she has ten silver coins and loses one of them? Won't she light a lamp, sweep the floor, and look carefully until she finds it? [9]Then she will call in her friends and neighbors and say, "Let's celebrate! I've found the coin I lost."

[10]Jesus said, "In the same way God's angels are happy when even one person turns to him."

[a]15.1 *Tax collectors:* These were usually Jewish people who paid the Romans for the right to collect taxes. They were hated by other Jews who thought of them as traitors to their country and to their religion.

Prayer Starter: May more and more people turn to you, O Lord.

Memory Verse: Look at the crows! They don't plant or harvest, and they don't have . . .
                                                                    —*Luke 12.24*

A Runaway Son Comes Home

Jesus also told them another story:

Once a man had two sons. ¹²The younger son said to his father, "Give me my share of the property." So the father divided his property between his two sons.

¹³Not long after that, the younger son packed up everything he owned and left for a foreign country, where he wasted all his money in wild living. ¹⁴He had spent everything, when a bad famine spread through that whole land. Soon he had nothing to eat.

¹⁵He went to work for a man in that country, and the man sent him out to take care of his pigs.ᵃ ¹⁶He would have been glad to eat what the pigs were eating,ᵇ but no one gave him a thing.

¹⁷Finally, he came to his senses and said, "My father's workers have plenty to eat, and here I am, starving to death! ¹⁸I will go to my father and say to him, 'Father, I have sinned against God in heaven and against you. ¹⁹I am no longer good enough to be called your son. Treat me like one of your workers.'"

²⁰The younger son got up and started back to his father. But when he was still a long way off, his father saw him and felt sorry for him. He ran to his son and hugged and kissed him.

²¹The son said, "Father, I have sinned against God in heaven and against you. I am no longer good enough to be called your son."

²²But his father said to the servants, "Hurry, and bring the best clothes and put them on him. Give him a ring for his finger and sandalsᶜ for his feet. ²³Get the best calf and prepare it, so we can eat and celebrate. ²⁴This son of mine was dead, but has now come back to life. He was lost and has now been found." And they began to celebrate.

²⁵The older son had been out in the field. But when he came near the house, he heard the music and dancing. ²⁶So he called one of the servants over and asked, "What's going on here?"

²⁷The servant answered, "Your brother has come home safe and sound, and your father ordered us to kill the best calf." ²⁸The older brother got so angry that he would not even go into the house.

His father came out and begged him to go in. ²⁹But he said to his father, "For years I have worked for you like a slave and have always obeyed you. But you have never even given me a little goat, so that I could give a dinner for my friends. ³⁰This other son of yours wasted your money on prostitutes. And now that he has come home, you ordered the best calf to be killed for a feast."

³¹His father replied, "My son, you are always with me, and everything I have is yours. ³²But we should be glad and celebrate! Your brother was dead, but he is now alive. He was lost and has now been found."

ᵃ15.15 *pigs:* The Jewish religion taught that pigs were not fit to eat or even to touch. A Jewish man would have felt terribly insulted if he had to feed pigs, much less eat with them. ᵇ15.16 *what the pigs were eating:* The Greek text has "(bean) pods," which came from a tree in Palestine. These were used to feed animals. Poor people sometimes ate them too. ᶜ15.22 *ring . . . sandals:* These show that the young man's father fully accepted him as his son. A ring was a sign of high position in the family. Sandals showed that he was a son instead of a slave, since slaves did not usually wear sandals.

Prayer Starter: Dear God, help us to love each other in our families.

Memory Verse: Look at the crows! They don't plant or harvest, and they don't have storehouses or barns. . . .   —*Luke 12.24*

Jesus told his disciples a story about how they should keep on praying and never give up:

A Widow and a Judge

²In a town there was once a judge who didn't fear God or care about people. ³In that same town there was a widow who kept going to the judge and saying, "Make sure that I get fair treatment in court."

⁴For a while the judge refused to do anything. Finally, he said to himself, "Even though I don't fear God or care about people, ⁵I will help this widow because she keeps on bothering me. If I don't help her, she will wear me out."

⁶The Lord said:

Think about what that crooked judge said. ⁷Won't God protect his chosen ones who pray to him day and night? Won't he be concerned for them? ⁸He will surely hurry and help them. But when the Son of Man comes, will he find on this earth anyone with faith?

19Jesus was going through Jericho, ²where a man named Zacchaeus lived. He was in charge of collecting taxes^a and was very rich. ³⁴Jesus was heading his way, and Zacchaeus wanted to see what he was like. But Zacchaeus was a short man and could not see over the crowd. So he ran ahead and climbed up into a sycamore tree.

⁵When Jesus got there, he looked up and said, "Zacchaeus, hurry down! I want to stay with you today." ⁶Zacchaeus hurried down and gladly welcomed Jesus.

⁷Everyone who saw this started grumbling, "This man Zacchaeus is a sinner! And Jesus is going home to eat with him."

⁸Later that day Zacchaeus stood up and said to the Lord, "I will give half of my property to the poor. And I will now pay back four times as much[b] to everyone I have ever cheated."

⁹Jesus said to Zacchaeus, "Today you and your family have been saved,[c] because you are a true son of Abraham.[d] ¹⁰The Son of Man came to look for and to save people who are lost."

---

[a]19.2 *in charge of collecting taxes:* Tax collectors were usually Jewish people who paid the Romans for the right to collect taxes. They were hated by other Jews who thought of them as traitors to their country and to their religion. [b]19.8 *pay back four times as much:* Both Jewish and Roman law said that a person must pay back four times the amount that was taken. [c]19.9 *saved:* Zacchaeus was Jewish, but it is only now that he is rescued from sin and placed under God's care. [d]19.9 *son of Abraham:* As used in this verse, the words mean that Zacchaeus is truly one of God's special people.

Prayer Starter: Help me to keep on praying, Lord, and never give up.

Memory Verse: Look at the crows! They don't plant or harvest, and they don't have storehouses or barns. But God takes care of them.

—Luke 12.24

Jesus Is Betrayed

Jesus went out to the Mount of Olives, as he often did, and his disciples went with him. ⁴⁰When they got there, he told them, "Pray that you won't be tested."

⁴¹Jesus walked on a little way before he knelt down and prayed, ⁴²"Father, if you will, please don't make me suffer by having me drink from this cup.ª But do what you want, and not what I want."

⁴³Then an angel from heaven came to help him. ⁴⁴Jesus was in great pain and prayed so sincerely that his sweat fell to the ground like drops of blood.ᵇ

⁴⁵Jesus got up from praying and went over to his disciples. They were asleep and worn out from being so sad. ⁴⁶He said to them, "Why are you asleep? Wake up and pray that you won't be tested."

⁴⁷While Jesus was still speaking, a crowd came up. It was led by Judas, one of the twelve apostles. He went over to Jesus and greeted him with a kiss.ᶜ

⁴⁸Jesus asked Judas, "Are you betraying the Son of Man with a kiss?"

⁴⁹When Jesus' disciples saw what was about to happen, they asked, "Lord, should we attack them with a sword?" ⁵⁰One of the disciples even struck at the high priest's servant with his sword and cut off the servant's right ear.

⁵¹"Enough of that!" Jesus said. Then he touched the servant's ear and healed it.

⁵²Jesus spoke to the chief priests, the temple police, and the leaders who had come to arrest him. He said, "Why do you come out with swords and clubs and treat me like a criminal? ⁵³I was with you every day in the temple, and you didn't arrest me. But this is your time, and darknessᵈ is in control."

ª22.42 *having me drink from this cup:* In the Scriptures "to drink from a cup" sometimes means to suffer. ᵇ22.43,44 *Then an angel . . . like drops of blood:* Verses 43,44 are not in some manuscripts. ᶜ22.47 *greeted him with a kiss:* It was the custom for people to greet each other with a kiss on the cheek. ᵈ22.53 *darkness:* Darkness stands for the power of the devil.

Prayer Starter: Lord, teach me to pray as Jesus did.

Memory Verse: He told them . . .   —*Luke 24.46*

Travelers to Emmaus

That same day two of Jesus' disciples were going to the village of Emmaus, which was about seven miles from Jerusalem. [14]As they were talking and thinking about what had happened, [15]Jesus came near and started walking along beside them. [16]But they did not know who he was.

[17]Jesus asked them, "What were you talking about as you walked along?"

The two of them stood there looking sad and gloomy. [18]Then the one named Cleopas asked Jesus, "Are you the only person from Jerusalem who didn't know what was happening there these last few days?"

[19]"What do you mean?" Jesus asked.

They answered:

Those things that happened to Jesus from Nazareth. By what he did and said he showed that he was a powerful prophet, who pleased God and all the people. [20]Then the chief priests and our leaders had him arrested and sentenced to die on a cross.

[25]Then Jesus asked the two disciples, "Why can't you understand? How can you be so slow to believe all that the prophets said? [26]Didn't you know that the Messiah would have to suffer before he was given his glory?" [27]Jesus then explained everything written about himself in the Scriptures, beginning with the Law of Moses and the Books of the Prophets.[a]

[a]24.27 *the Law of Moses and the Books of the Prophets:* See the note at 16.16.

Prayer Starter: I'm so glad Jesus is alive, Lord! Hallelujah!

Memory Verse: He told them: "The Scriptures say . . ." —*Luke 24.46*

Jesus Returns to Heaven

While Jesus' disciples were talking about what had happened, Jesus appeared and greeted them. ³⁷They were frightened and terrified because they thought they were seeing a ghost.

³⁸But Jesus said, "Why are you so frightened? Why do you doubt? ³⁹Look at my hands and my feet and see who I am! Touch me and find out for yourselves. Ghosts don't have flesh and bones as you see I have."

⁴⁰After Jesus said this, he showed them his hands and his feet. ⁴¹The disciples were so glad and amazed that they could not believe it. Jesus then asked them, "Do you have something to eat?" ⁴²They gave him a piece of baked fish. ⁴³He took it and ate it as they watched.

⁴⁴Jesus said to them, "While I was still with you, I told you that everything written about me in the Law of Moses, the Books of the Prophets, and in the Psalms[a] had to happen."

⁴⁵Then he helped them understand the Scriptures. ⁴⁶He told them:

The Scriptures say that the Messiah must suffer, then three days later he will rise from death. ⁴⁷They also say that all people of every nation must be told in my name to turn to God, in order to be forgiven. So beginning in Jerusalem, ⁴⁸you must tell everything that has happened. ⁴⁹I will send you the one my Father has promised,[b] but you must stay in the city until you are given power from heaven.

⁵⁰Jesus led his disciples out to Bethany, where he raised his hands and blessed them. ⁵¹As he was doing this, he left and was taken up to heaven.[c]

[a]24.44 *Psalms:* The Jewish Scriptures were made up of three parts: (1) the Law of Moses, (2) the Books of the Prophets, and (3) the Writings, which included the Psalms. Sometimes the Scriptures were just called the Law or the Law (of Moses) and the Books of the Prophets. [b]24.49 *the one my Father has promised:* Jesus means the Holy Spirit. [c]24.51 *and was taken up to heaven:* These words are not in some manuscripts.

Prayer Starter: Dear God, help me to understand the Bible better.

Memory Verse: He told them: "The Scriptures say that the Messiah must suffer . . ."   —*Luke 24.46*

A Wedding in Cana

Three days later Mary, the mother of Jesus, was at a wedding feast in the village of Cana in Galilee. [2]Jesus and his disciples had also been invited and were there.

[3]When the wine was all gone, Mary said to Jesus, "They don't have any more wine."

[4]Jesus replied, "Mother, my time hasn't yet come![a] You must not tell me what to do."

[5]Mary then said to the servants, "Do whatever Jesus tells you to do."

[6]At the feast there were six stone water jars that were used by the people for washing themselves in the way that their religion said they must. Each jar held about twenty or thirty gallons. [7]Jesus told the servants to fill them to the top with water. Then after the jars had been filled, [8]he said, "Now take some water and give it to the man in charge of the feast."

The servants did as Jesus told them, [9]and the man in charge drank some of the water that had now turned into wine. He did not know where the wine had come from, but the servants did. He called the bridegroom over [10]and said, "The best wine is always served first. Then after the guests have had plenty, the other wine is served. But you have kept the best until last!"

[11]This was Jesus' first miracle,[b] and he did it in the village of Cana in Galilee. There Jesus showed his glory, and his disciples put their faith in him. [12]After this, he went with his mother, his brothers, and his disciples to the town of Capernaum, where they stayed for a few days.

[a]2.4 *my time hasn't yet come!:* The time when the true glory of Jesus would be seen, and he would be recognized as God's Son. [b]2.11 *miracle:* The Greek text has "sign." In the Gospel of John the word "sign" is used for the miracle itself and as a way of pointing to Jesus as the Son of God.

Prayer Starter: Help me to do whatever Jesus tells me to, Lord.

Memory Verse: He told them: "The Scriptures say that the Messiah must suffer, then three days later he will rise . . . —*Luke 24.46*

Jesus in the Temple

Not long before the Jewish festival of Passover, Jesus went to Jerusalem. ¹⁴There he found people selling cattle, sheep, and doves in the temple. He also saw moneychangers sitting at their tables. ¹⁵So he took some rope and made a whip. Then he chased everyone out of the temple, together with their sheep and cattle. He turned over the tables of the money-changers and scattered their coins.

¹⁶Jesus said to the people who had been selling doves, "Get those doves out of here! Don't make my Father's house a marketplace."

¹⁷The disciples then remembered that the Scriptures say, "My love for your house burns in me like a fire."

¹⁸The Jewish leaders asked Jesus, "What miracle[a] will you work to show us why you have done this?"

¹⁹"Destroy this temple," Jesus answered, "and in three days I will build it again!"

²⁰The leaders replied, "It took forty-six years to build this temple. What makes you think you can rebuild it in three days?"

²¹But Jesus was talking about his body as a temple. ²²And when he was raised from death, his disciples remembered what he had told them. Then they believed the Scriptures and the words of Jesus.

---

[a]2.18 *miracle:* The Greek text has "sign." In the Gospel of John the word "sign" is used for the miracle itself and as a way of pointing to Jesus as the Son of God.

Prayer Starter: Lord, remind me to always show respect when I go into your church to worship.

Memory Verse: He told them: "The Scriptures say that the Messiah must suffer, then three days later he will rise from death." —*Luke 24.46*

Nicodemus Visits Jesus

There was a man named Nicodemus who was a Pharisee and a Jewish leader. ²One night he went to Jesus and said, "Sir, we know that God has sent you to teach us. You could not work these miracles, unless God were with you."

³Jesus replied, "I tell you for certain that you must be born from above[a] before you can see God's kingdom!"

⁴Nicodemus asked, "How can a grown man ever be born a second time?"

⁵Jesus answered:

I tell you for certain that before you can get into God's kingdom, you must be born not only by water, but by the Spirit. ⁶Humans give life to their children. Yet only God's Spirit can change you into a child of God. ⁷Don't be surprised when I say that you must be born from above. ⁸Only God's Spirit gives new life. The Spirit is like the wind that blows wherever it wants to. You can hear the wind, but you don't know where it comes from or where it is going.

⁹"How can this be?" Nicodemus asked.

¹⁰Jesus replied:

How can you be a teacher of Israel and not know these things? ¹¹I tell you for certain that we know what we are talking about because we have seen it ourselves. But none of you will accept what we say. ¹²If you don't believe when I talk to you about things on earth, how can you possibly believe if I talk to you about things in heaven?

[a]3.3 *from above:* Or "in a new way."

Prayer Starter: Thank you, God, for loving the people of this world enough to give your only Son to save them.

Memory Verse: God loved the people of this world so much . . .

—John 3.16

The Woman at the Well

Jesus left Judea and started for Galilee again. ⁴This time he had to go through Samaria, ⁵and on his way he came to the town of Sychar. It was near the field that Jacob had long ago given to his son Joseph. ⁶⁻⁸The well that Jacob had dug was still there, and Jesus sat down beside it because he was tired from traveling. It was noon, and after Jesus' disciples had gone into town to buy some food, a Samaritan woman came to draw water from the well.

Jesus asked her, "Would you please give me a drink of water?"

⁹"You are a Jew," she replied, "and I am a Samaritan woman. How can you ask me for a drink of water when Jews and Samaritans won't have anything to do with each other?"ᵃ

¹⁰Jesus answered, "You don't know what God wants to give you, and you don't know who is asking you for a drink. If you did, you would ask me for the water that gives life."

¹¹"Sir," the woman said, "you don't even have a bucket, and the well is deep. Where are you going to get this life-giving water? ¹²Our ancestor Jacob dug this well for us, and his family and animals got water from it. Are you greater than Jacob?"

¹³Jesus answered, "Everyone who drinks this water will get thirsty again. ¹⁴But no one who drinks the water I give will ever be thirsty again. The water I give is like a flowing fountain that gives eternal life."

ᵃ4.9 *won't have anything to do with each other:* Or "won't use the same cups." The Samaritans lived in the land between Judea and Galilee. They worshiped God differently from the Jews and did not get along with them.

Prayer Starter: You give me the water of life, Lord. Thank you.

Memory Verse: God loved the people of this world so much that he gave his only Son . . .
            —*John 3.16*

Jesus' Brothers

Jesus decided to leave Judea and to start going through Galilee because the leaders of the people wanted to kill him. ²It was almost time for the Festival of Shelters, ³and Jesus' brothers said to him, "Why don't you go to Judea? Then your disciples can see what you are doing. ⁴No one does anything in secret, if they want others to know about them. So let the world know what you are doing!" ⁵Even Jesus' own brothers had not yet become his followers.

⁶Jesus answered, "My time hasn't yet come,ᵃ but your time is always here. ⁷The people of this world cannot hate you. They hate me, because I tell them that they do evil things. ⁸Go on to the festival. My time hasn't yet come, and I am not going." ⁹Jesus said this and stayed on in Galilee.

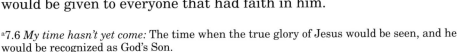

¹⁰After Jesus' brothers had gone to the festival, he went secretly, without telling anyone.

¹¹During the festival the leaders looked for Jesus and asked, "Where is he?" ¹²The crowds even got into an argument about him. Some were saying, "Jesus is a good man," while others were saying, "He is lying to everyone." ¹³But the people were afraid of their leaders, and none of them talked in public about him.

³⁷On the last and most important day of the festival, Jesus stood up and shouted, "If you are thirsty, come to me and drink! ³⁸Have faith in me, and you will have life-giving water flowing from deep inside you, just as the Scriptures say." ³⁹Jesus was talking about the Holy Spirit, who would be given to everyone that had faith in him.

ᵃ7.6 *My time hasn't yet come:* The time when the true glory of Jesus would be seen, and he would be recognized as God's Son.

Prayer Starter: Father, help me to share the water of life with others.

Memory Verse: God loved the people of this world so much that he gave his only Son, so that everyone who has faith . . .   *—John 3.16*

The Blind Man

As Jesus walked along, he saw a man who had been blind since birth. ²Jesus' disciples asked, "Teacher, why was this man born blind? Was it because he or his parents sinned?"

³"No, it wasn't!" Jesus answered. "But because of his blindness, you will see God work a miracle for him.

⁴As long as it is day, we must do what the one who sent me wants me to do. When night comes, no one can work. ⁵While I am in the world, I am the light for the world."

⁶After Jesus said this, he spit on the ground. He made some mud and smeared it on the man's eyes. ⁷Then he said, "Go and wash off the mud in Siloam Pool." The man went and washed in Siloam, which means "One Who Is Sent." When he had washed off the mud, he could see.

⁸The man's neighbors and the people who had seen him begging wondered if he really could be the same man. ⁹Some of them said he was the same beggar, while others said he only looked like him. But he told them, "I am that man."

[10]"Then how can you see?" they asked.

[11]He answered, "Someone named Jesus made some mud and smeared it on my eyes. He told me to go and wash it off in Siloam Pool. When I did, I could see."

[12]"Where is he now?" they asked.

"I don't know," he answered.

[13-14]The day when Jesus made the mud and healed the man was a Sabbath. So the people took the man to the Pharisees. [15]They asked him how he was able to see, and he answered, "Jesus made some mud and smeared it on my eyes. Then after I washed it off, I could see."

[16]Some of the Pharisees said, "This man Jesus doesn't come from God. If he did, he would not break the law of the Sabbath."

Others asked, "How could someone who is a sinner work such a miracle?"[a]

Since the Pharisees could not agree among themselves, [17]they asked the man, "What do you say about this one who healed your eyes?"

"He is a prophet!" the man told them.

[24]The leaders called the man back and said, "Swear by God to tell the truth! We know that Jesus is a sinner."

[25]The man replied, "I don't know if he is a sinner or not. All I know is that I used to be blind, but now I can see!"

---

[a]9.16 *miracle:* The Greek text has "sign." In the Gospel of John the word "sign" is used for the miracle itself and as a way of pointing to Jesus as the Son of God.

Prayer Starter: I'm amazed at Jesus' power! I praise and worship him.

Memory Verse: God loved the people of this world so much that he gave his only Son, so that everyone who has faith in him will have eternal life . . .
—*John 3.16*

The Good Shepherd

Jesus said:

I tell you for certain that I am the gate for the sheep. ⁸Everyone who came before me was a thief or a robber, and the sheep did not listen to any of them. ⁹I am the gate. All who came in through me will be saved. Through me they will come and go and find pasture.

¹⁰A thief comes only to rob, kill and destroy. I came so that everyone would have life, and have it in its fullest. ¹¹I am the good shepherd, and the good shepherd gives up his life for his sheep. ¹²Hired workers are not like the shepherd. They don't own the sheep, and when they see a wolf coming, they run off and leave the sheep. Then the wolf attacks and scatters the flock. ¹³Hired workers run away because they don't care about the sheep.

¹⁴I am the good shepherd. I know my sheep, and they know me. ¹⁵Just as the Father knows me, I know the Father, and I give up my life for my sheep. ¹⁶I have other sheep that are not in this sheep pen. I must bring them together too, when they hear my voice. Then there will be one flock of sheep and one shepherd.

Prayer Starter: Lord, give me life to the fullest!

Memory Verse: God loved the people of this world so much that he gave his only Son, so that everyone who has faith in him will have eternal life and never really die.

—*John 3.16*

Lazarus, Come Out!

Jesus then said, "I am the one who raises the dead to life! Everyone who has faith in me will live, even if they die. ²⁶And everyone who lives because of faith in me will never really die. Do you believe this?"

²⁷"Yes, Lord!" she replied. "I believe that you are Christ, the Son of God. You are the one we hoped would come into the world."

²⁸After Martha said this, she went and privately said to her sister Mary, "The Teacher is here, and he wants to see you." ²⁹As soon as Mary heard this, she got up and went out to Jesus. ³⁰He was still outside the village where Martha had gone to meet him. ³¹Many people had come to comfort Mary, and when they saw her quickly leave the house, they thought she was going out to the tomb to cry. So they followed her.

³²Mary went to where Jesus was. Then as soon as she saw him, she knelt at his feet and said, "Lord, if you had been here, my brother would not have died."

³³When Jesus saw that Mary and the people with her were crying, he was terribly upset ³⁴and asked, "Where have you put his body?"

They replied, "Lord, come and you will see."

³⁵Jesus started crying, ³⁶and the people said, "See how much he loved Lazarus."

³⁷Some of them said, "He gives sight to the blind. Why couldn't he have kept Lazarus from dying?"

³⁸Jesus was still terribly upset. So he went to the tomb, which was a cave with a stone rolled against the entrance. ³⁹Then he told the people to roll the stone away. But Martha said, "Lord, you know that Lazarus has been dead four days, and there will be a bad smell."

⁴⁰Jesus replied, "Didn't I tell you that if you had faith, you would see the glory of God?"

⁴¹After the stone had been rolled aside, Jesus looked up toward heaven and prayed, "Father, I thank you for answering my prayer. ⁴²I know that you always answer my prayers. But I said this, so that the people here would believe that you sent me."

⁴³When Jesus had finished praying, he shouted, "Lazarus, come out!" ⁴⁴The man who had been dead came out. His hands and feet were wrapped with strips of burial cloth, and a cloth covered his face.

Jesus then told the people, "Untie him and let him go."

Prayer Starter: Father, I thank you for answering my prayers.

Memory Verse: Jesus then said . . .   *—John 11.25*

Washing Feet

It was before Passover, and Jesus knew that the time had come for him to leave this world and to return to the Father. He had always loved his followers in this world, and he loved them to the very end.

²Even before the evening meal started, the devil had made Judas, the son of Simon Iscariot,ᵃ decide to betray Jesus.

³Jesus knew that he had come from God and would go back to God. He also knew that the Father had given him complete power. ⁴So during the meal Jesus got up, removed his outer garment, and wrapped a towel around his waist. ⁵He put some water into a large bowl. Then he began washing his disciples' feet and drying them with the towel he was wearing.

⁶But when he came to Simon Peter, that disciple asked, "Lord, are you going to wash my feet?"

⁷Jesus answered, "You don't really know what I am doing, but later you will understand."

⁸"You will never wash my feet!" Peter replied.

"If I don't wash you," Jesus told him, "you don't really belong to me."

⁹Peter said, "Lord, don't wash just my feet. Wash my hands and my head."

[10]Jesus answered, "People who have bathed and are clean all over need to wash just their feet. And you, my disciples, are clean, except for one of you." [11]Jesus knew who would betray him. That is why he said, "except for one of you."

[12]After Jesus had washed his disciples' feet and had put his outer garment back on, he sat down again.[b] Then he said:

> Do you understand what I have done? [13]You call me your teacher and Lord, and you should, because that is who I am. [14]And if your Lord and teacher has washed your feet, you should do the same for each other. [15]I have set the example, and you should do for each other exactly what I have done for you. [16]I tell you for certain that servants are not greater than their master, and messengers are not greater than the one who sent them. [17]You know these things, and God will bless you, if you do them.

[a]13.2 *Iscariot:* This may mean "a man from Kerioth" (a place in Judea). But more probably it means "a man who was a liar" or "a man who was a betrayer." [b]13.12 *sat down again:* On special occasions the Jewish people followed the Greek and Roman custom of lying down on their left side and leaning on their left elbow while eating with their right hand.

Prayer Starter: Make me a humble servant, just like the Lord Jesus.

Memory Verse: Jesus then said, "I am the one . . ."   —*John 11.25*

Jesus Is Arrested

When Jesus had finished praying, he and his disciples crossed the Kidron Valley and went into a garden.[a] [2]Jesus had often met there with his disciples, and Judas knew where the place was.

[3-5]Judas had promised to betray Jesus. So he went to the garden with some Roman soldiers and temple police, who had been sent by the chief priests and the Pharisees. They carried torches, lanterns, and weapons. Jesus already knew everything that was going to happen, but he asked, "Who are you looking for?"

They answered, "We are looking for Jesus from Nazareth!"

Jesus told them, "I am Jesus!"[b] [6]At once they all backed away and fell to the ground.

[7]Jesus again asked, "Who are you looking for?"

"We are looking for Jesus from Nazareth," they answered.

[8]This time Jesus replied, "I have already told you that I am Jesus. If I am the one you are looking for, let these others go. [9]Then everything will happen, just as the Scriptures say, 'I did not lose anyone you gave me.'"

[10]Simon Peter had brought along a sword. He now pulled it out and struck at the servant of the high priest. The servant's name was Malchus, and Peter cut off his right ear. [11]Jesus told Peter, "Put your sword away. I must drink from the cup[c] that the Father has given me."

[12]The Roman officer and his men, together with the temple police, arrested Jesus and tied him up.

[a]18.1 *garden:* The Greek word is usually translated "garden," but probably referred to an olive orchard. [b]18.3-5 *I am Jesus:* The Greek text has "I am." [c]18.11 *drink from the cup:* In the Scriptures a cup is sometimes used as a symbol of suffering. To "drink from the cup" is to suffer.

Prayer Starter: Help me to be patient, Lord, with people I don't like.

Memory Verse: Jesus then said, "I am the one who raises the dead to life! . . ."
—*John 11.25*

King of the Jews

Pilate ordered the charge against Jesus to be written on a board and put above the cross. It read, "Jesus of Nazareth, King of the Jews." [20]The words were written in Hebrew, Latin, and Greek.

The place where Jesus was taken wasn't far from the city, and many of the people read the charge against him. [21]So the chief priests went to Pilate and said, "Why did you write that he is King of the Jews? You should have written, 'He claimed to be King of the Jews.'"

[22]But Pilate told them, "What is written will not be changed!"

[23]After the soldiers had nailed Jesus to the cross, they divided up his clothes into four parts, one for each of them. But his outer garment was made from a single piece of cloth, and it did not have any seams. [24]The soldiers said to each other, "Let's not rip it apart. We will gamble to see who gets it." This happened so that the Scriptures would come true, which say,

"They divided up my clothes
and gambled for my garments."

The soldiers then did what they had decided.

[25]Jesus' mother stood beside his cross with her sister and Mary the wife of Clopas. Mary Magdalene was standing there too.[a] [26]When Jesus saw his mother and his favorite disciple with her, he said to his mother, "This man is now your son." [27]Then he said to the disciple, "She is now your mother." From then on, that disciple took her into his own home.

[28]Jesus knew that he had now finished his work. And in order to make the Scriptures come true, he said, "I am thirsty!" [29]A jar of cheap wine was there. Someone then soaked a sponge with the wine and held it up to Jesus' mouth on the stem of a hyssop plant. [30]After Jesus drank the wine, he said, "Everything is done!" He bowed his head and died.

[a]19.25 *Jesus' mother stood beside his cross with her sister and Mary the wife of Clopas. Mary Magdalene was standing there too:* The Greek text may also be understood to include only three women ("Jesus' mother stood beside the cross with her sister, Mary the mother of Clopas. Mary Magdalene was standing there too.") or merely two women ("Jesus' mother was standing there with her sister Mary of Clopas, that is Mary Magdalene."). "Of Clopas" may mean "daughter of" or "mother of."

Prayer Starter: Thank you for the cross of Jesus, and for the empty tomb.

Memory Verse: Jesus then said, "I am the one who raises the dead to life! Everyone who has faith in me will live . . ." —*John 11.25*

Jesus of Nazareth
King of the Jews

The Empty Tomb

J oseph from Arimathea was one of Jesus' disciples. He had kept it secret though, because he was afraid of the Jewish leaders. But now he asked Pilate to let him have Jesus' body. Pilate gave him permission, and Joseph took it down from the cross.

[39]Nicodemus also came with about seventy-five pounds of spices made from myrrh and aloes. This was the same Nicodemus who had visited Jesus one night. [40]The two men

wrapped the body in a linen cloth, together with the spices, which was how the Jewish people buried their dead. [41]In the place where Jesus had been nailed to a cross, there was a garden with a tomb that had never been used. [42]The tomb was nearby, and since it was the time to prepare for the Sabbath, they were in a hurry to put Jesus' body there.

20 On Sunday morning while it was still dark, Mary Magdalene went to the tomb and saw that the stone had been rolled away from the entrance. [2]She ran to Simon Peter and to Jesus' favorite disciple and said, "They have taken the Lord from the tomb! We don't know where they have put him."

[3]Peter and the other disciple started for the tomb. [4]They ran side by

side, until the other disciple ran faster than Peter and got there first. ⁵He bent over and saw the strips of linen cloth lying inside the tomb, but he did not go in.

⁶When Simon Peter got there, he went into the tomb and saw the strips of cloth. ⁷He also saw the piece of cloth that had been used to cover Jesus' face. It was rolled up and in a place by itself. ⁸The disciple who got there first then went into the tomb, and when he saw it, he believed. ⁹At that time Peter and the other disciple did not know that the Scriptures said Jesus would rise to life. ¹⁰So the two of them went back to the other disciples.

Prayer Starter: Remind me each day, Lord, that Jesus is alive.

Memory Verse: Jesus then said, "I am the one who raises the dead to life! Everyone who has faith in me will live, even if they die." —*John 11.25*

Jesus Appears to Mary

Mary Magdalene stood crying outside the tomb. She was still weeping, when she stooped down ¹²and saw two angels inside. They were dressed in white and were sitting where Jesus' body had been. One was at the head and the other was at the foot. ¹³The angels asked Mary, "Why are you crying?"

She answered, "They have taken away my Lord's body! I don't know where they have put him."

¹⁴As soon as Mary said this, she turned around and saw Jesus standing there. But she did not know who he was. ¹⁵Jesus asked her, "Why are you crying? Who are you looking for?"

She thought he was the gardener and said, "Sir, if you have taken his body away, please tell me, so I can go and get him."

¹⁶Then Jesus said to her, "Mary!"

She turned and said to him. "Rabboni." The Aramaic word "Rabboni" means "Teacher."

¹⁷Jesus told her, "Don't hold on to me! I have not yet gone to the Father. But tell my disciples that I am going to the one who is my Father and my God, as well as your Father and your God." ¹⁸Mary Magdalene then went and told the disciples that she had seen the Lord. She also told them what he had said to her.

Prayer Starter: Help me to tell others the good news that Jesus rose from the dead.

Memory Verse: But the Holy Spirit will come upon you . . . *—Acts 1.8*

Jesus and Thomas

The disciples were afraid of the Jewish leaders, and on the evening of that same Sunday they locked themselves in a room. Suddenly, Jesus appeared in the middle of the group. He greeted them ²⁰and showed them his hands and his side. When the disciples saw the Lord, they became very happy.

²¹After Jesus had greeted them again, he said, "I am sending you, just as the Father has sent me." ²²Then he breathed on them and said, "Receive the Holy Spirit. ²³If you forgive anyone's sins, they will be forgiven. But if you don't forgive their sins, they will not be forgiven."

²⁴Although Thomas the Twin was one of the twelve disciples, he wasn't with the others when Jesus appeared to them. ²⁵So they told him, "We have seen the Lord!"

But Thomas said, "First, I must see the nail scars in his hands and touch them with my finger. I must put my hand where the spear went into his side. I won't believe unless I do this!"

²⁶A week later the disciples were together again. This time, Thomas was with them. Jesus came in while the doors were still locked and stood in the middle of the group. He greeted his disciples ²⁷and said to Thomas, "Put your finger here and look at my hands! Put your hand into my side. Stop doubting and have faith!"

²⁸Thomas replied, "You are my Lord and my God!"

Prayer Starter: Thank you, heavenly Father, for Jesus who is my Lord and my God.

Memory Verse: But the Holy Spirit will come upon you and give you power. . . .
—*Acts 1.8*

Two Men Dressed in White

For forty days after Jesus had suffered and died, he proved in many ways that he had been raised from death. He appeared to his apostles and spoke to them about God's kingdom. ⁴While he was still with them, he said:

Don't leave Jerusalem yet. Wait here for the Father to give you the Holy Spirit, just as I told you he has promised to do. ⁵John baptized with water, but in a few days you will be baptized with the Holy Spirit.

⁶While the apostles were still with Jesus, they asked him, "Lord, are you now going to give Israel its own king again."ᵃ

⁷Jesus said to them, "You don't need to know the time of those events that only the Father controls. ⁸But the Holy Spirit will come upon you and give you power. Then you will tell everyone about me in Jerusalem, in all Judea, in Samaria, and everywhere in the world." ⁹After Jesus had said this and while they were watching, he was taken up into a cloud. They could not see him, ¹⁰but as he went up, they kept looking up into the sky.

Suddenly two men dressed in white clothes were standing there beside them. ¹¹They said, "Why are you men from Galilee standing here and looking up into the sky? Jesus has been taken to heaven. But he will come back in the same way that you have seen him go."

ᵃ1.6 *are you now going to give Israel its own king again?:* Or "Are you now going to rule Israel as its king?"

Prayer Starter: Please hurry and come back to earth, Lord. We love you.

Memory Verse: But the Holy Spirit will come upon you and give you power. Then you will tell everyone about me in Jerusalem . . .

—*Acts 1.8*

The Disciples Meet

After the apostles returned to the city, they went upstairs to the room where they had been staying.

[14]The apostles often met together and prayed with a single purpose in mind.[a] The women and Mary the mother of Jesus would meet with them, and so would his brothers. [15]One day there were about one hundred twenty of the Lord's followers meeting together, and Peter stood up to speak to them. [16-17]He said:

My friends, long ago by the power of the Holy Spirit, David said something about Judas, and what he said has now happened. Judas was one of us and had worked with us, but he brought the mob to arrest Jesus.

[21-22]So we need someone else to help us tell others that Jesus has been raised from death. He must also be one of the men who was with us from the very beginning. He must have been with us from the time the Lord Jesus was baptized by John until the day he was taken to heaven.

[23]Two men were suggested: One of them was Joseph Barsabbas, known as Justus, and the other was Matthias. [24]Then they all prayed, "Lord, you know what everyone is like! Show us the one you have chosen [25]to be an apostle and to serve in place of Judas, who got what he deserved." [26]They drew names, and Matthias was chosen to join the group of the eleven apostles.

[a]1.14 *met together and prayed with a single purpose in mind:* Or "met together in a special place for prayer."

Prayer Starter: Show me your choices for me, each day, O Lord.

Memory Verse: But the Holy Spirit will come upon you and give you power. Then you will tell everyone about me in Jerusalem, in all Judea, in Samaria . . .
                                                                    —*Acts 1.8*

The Day of Pentecost

On the day of Pentecost[a] all the Lord's followers were together in one place. ²Suddenly there was a noise from heaven like the sound of a mighty wind! It filled the house where they were meeting. ³Then they saw what looked like fiery tongues moving in all directions, and a tongue came and settled on each person there. ⁴The Holy Spirit took control of everyone, and they began speaking whatever languages the Spirit let them speak.

⁵Many religious Jews from every country in the world were living in Jerusalem. ⁶And when they heard this noise, a crowd gathered. But they were surprised, because they were hearing everything in their own languages. ⁷They were excited and amazed, and said:

Don't all these who are speaking come from Galilee? ⁸Then why do we hear them speaking our very own languages? ⁹Some of us are from Parthia, Media, and Elam. Others are from Mesopotamia, Judea, Cappadocia, Pontus, Asia, ¹⁰Phrygia, Pamphylia, Egypt, parts of Libya near Cyrene, Rome, ¹¹Crete, and Arabia. Some of us were born Jews, and others of us have chosen to be Jews. Yet we all hear them using our own languages to tell the wonderful things God has done.

[a]2.1 *Pentecost:* A Jewish festival that came fifty days after Passover and celebrated the wheat harvest. Jews later celebrated Pentecost as the time when they were given the Law of Moses.

Prayer Starter: Thank you for giving me a tongue for speaking. Help me to use it to share Christ with others.

Memory Verse: But the Holy Spirit will come upon you and give you power. Then you will tell everyone about me in Jerusalem, in all Judea, in Samaria, and everywhere in the world. —*Acts 1.8*

Peter Heals a Lame Man

The time of prayer[a] was about three o'clock in the afternoon, and Peter and John were going into the temple. [2]A man who had been born lame was being carried to the temple door. Each day he was placed beside this door, known as the Beautiful Gate. He sat there and begged from the people who were going in.

[3]The man saw Peter and John entering the temple, and he asked them for money. [4]But they looked straight at him and said, "Look up at us!"

[5]The man stared at them and thought he was going to get something. [6]But Peter said, "I don't have any silver or gold! But I will give you what I do have. In the name of Jesus Christ from Nazareth, get up and start walking." [7]Peter then took him by the right hand and helped him up.

At once the man's feet and ankles became strong, [8]and he jumped up and started walking. He went with Peter and John into the temple, walking and jumping and praising God. [9]Everyone saw him walking around and praising God. [10]They knew that he was the beggar who had been lying beside the Beautiful Gate, and they were completely surprised. They could not imagine what had happened to the man.

[a]3.1 *The time of prayer:* Many of the Jewish people prayed in their homes at regular times each day, and on special occasions they prayed in the temple.

Prayer Starter: Thank you for my feet and legs. Thank you for giving me energy each day.

Memory Verse: Only Jesus has the power . . . —*Acts 4.12*

Peter and John Arrested

The apostles were still talking to the people, when some priests, the captain of the temple guard, and some Sadducees arrived. ²These men were angry because the apostles were teaching the people that the dead would be raised from death, just as Jesus had been raised from death. ³It was already late in the afternoon, and they arrested Peter and John and put them in jail for the night. ⁴But a lot of people who had heard the message believed it. So by now there were about five thousand followers of the Lord.

⁵The next morning the leaders, the elders, and the teachers of the Law of Moses met in Jerusalem. ⁶The high priest Annas was there, as well as Caiaphas, John, Alexander, and other members of the high priest's family. ⁷They brought in Peter and John and made them stand in the middle while they questioned them. They asked, "By what power and in whose name have you done this?"

⁸Peter was filled with the Holy Spirit and told the nation's leaders and the elders:

⁹You are questioning us today about a kind deed in which a crippled man was healed. ¹⁰But there is something we must tell you and

everyone else in Israel. This man is standing here completely well because of the power of Jesus Christ from Nazareth. You put Jesus to death on a cross, but God raised him to life. ¹¹He is the stone that you builders thought was worthless, and now he is the most important stone of all. ¹²Only Jesus has the power to save! His name is the only one in all the world that can save anyone.

¹³The officials were amazed to see how brave Peter and John were, and they knew that these two apostles were only ordinary men and not well educated. The officials were certain that these men had been with Jesus. ¹⁴But they could not deny what had happened. The man who had been healed was standing there with the apostles.

¹⁵The officials commanded them to leave the council room. Then the officials said to each other, ¹⁶"What can we do with these men? Everyone in Jerusalem knows about this miracle, and we cannot say it didn't happen. ¹⁷But to keep this thing from spreading, we will warn them never again to speak to anyone about the name of Jesus." ¹⁸So they called the two apostles back in and told them that they must never, for any reason, teach anything about the name of Jesus.

¹⁹Peter and John answered, "Do you think God wants us to obey you or to obey him? ²⁰We cannot keep quiet about what we have seen and heard."

²¹⁻²²The officials could not find any reason to punish Peter and John. So they threatened them and let them go. The man who was healed by this miracle was more than forty years old, and everyone was praising God for what had happened.

Prayer Starter: Lord, your name is the only one in all the earth that can save anyone.

<table>
<tr><td>

**Ananias
and
Sapphira**

</td><td>

Joseph was one of the followers who had sold a piece of property and brought the money to the apostles. He was a Levite from Cyprus, and the apostles called him Barnabas, which means, "one who encourages others."

</td></tr>
</table>

5 Ananias and his wife Sapphira also sold a piece of property. ²But they agreed to cheat and keep some of the money for themselves.

So when Ananias took the rest of the money to the apostles, ³Peter said, "Why has Satan made you keep back some of the money from the sale of the property? Why have you lied to the Holy Spirit? ⁴The property was yours before you sold it, and even after you sold it, the money was still yours. What made you do such a thing? You didn't lie to people. You lied to God!"

⁵As soon as Ananias heard this, he dropped dead, and everyone who heard about it was frightened. ⁶Some young men came in and wrapped up his body. Then they took it out and buried it.

⁷Three hours later Sapphira came in, but she did not know what had happened to her husband. ⁸Peter asked her, "Tell me, did you sell the property for this amount?"

"Yes," she answered, "that's the amount."

⁹Then Peter said, "Why did the two of you agree to test the Lord's Spirit? The men who buried Ananias are by the door, and they will carry you out!" ¹⁰At once she fell at Peter's feet and died.

When the young men came back in, they found Sapphira lying there dead. So they carried her out and buried her beside her husband. ¹¹The church members were afraid, and so was everyone else who heard what had happened.

Prayer Starter: Help me always be honest, Lord. Keep me from cheating and lying.

Memory Verse: Only Jesus has the power to save! His name is the only one . . .
—*Acts 4.12*

Many Miracles

The apostles worked many miracles and wonders among the people. All of the Lord's followers often met in the part of the temple known as Solomon's Porch.ᵃ ¹³No one outside their group dared join them, even though everyone liked them very much.

¹⁴Many men and women started having faith in the Lord. ¹⁵Then sick people were brought out to the road and placed on cots and mats. It was hoped that Peter would walk by, and

his shadow would fall on them and heal them. ¹⁶A lot of people living in the towns near Jerusalem brought those who were sick or troubled by evil spirits, and they were all healed.

¹⁷The high priest and all the other Sadducees who were with him became jealous. ¹⁸They arrested the apostles and put them in the city jail. ¹⁹But that night an angel from the Lord opened the doors of the jail and led the apostles out. The angel said, ²⁰"Go to the temple and tell the people everything about this new life." ²¹So they went into the temple before sunrise and started teaching.

The high priest and his men called together their council, which included all of Israel's leaders. Then they ordered the apostles to be brought to them from the jail. ²²The temple police who were sent to the jail did not find the apostles. They returned and said, ²³"We found the jail locked tight and the guards standing at the doors. But when we opened the doors and went in we didn't find anyone there." [24]The captain of the temple police and the chief priests listened to their report, but they did not know what to think about it.

[25]Just then someone came in and said, "Right now those men you put in jail are in the temple, teaching the people!" [26]The captain went with some of the temple police and brought the apostles back. But they did not use force. They were afraid that the people might start throwing stones at them.

[a]5.12 *Solomon's Porch:* A public place with tall columns along the east side of the temple.

Prayer Starter: Thank you, Lord, for the angels who watch over us.

Memory Verse: Only Jesus has the power to save! His name is the only one in all the world . . .   *—Acts 4.12*

Apostles Beaten

When the apostles were brought before the council, the high priest said to them, [28]"We told you plainly not to teach in the name of Jesus. But look what you have done! You have been teaching all over Jerusalem, and you are trying to blame us for his death."

[29]Peter and the apostles replied:

We don't obey people. We obey God. [30]You killed Jesus by nailing him to a cross. But the God our ancestors worshiped raised him to life [31]and made him our Leader and Savior. Then God gave him a place at his right side,[a] so that the people of Israel would turn back to him and be forgiven. [32]We are here to tell you about all this, and so is the Holy Spirit, who is God's gift to everyone who obeys God.

[33]When the council members heard this, they became so angry that they wanted to kill the apostles. [34]But one of the members was the Pharisee Gamaliel, a highly respected teacher. He ordered the apostles to be taken out of the room for a little while. [35]Then he said to the council:

Be careful what you do with these men. [36]Not long ago Theudas claimed to be someone inportant, and about four hundred men joined him. But he was killed. All his followers were scattered, and that was the end of that.

[37]Later, when the people of our nation were being counted, Judas from Galilee showed up. A lot of people followed him, but he was killed, and all his followers were scattered.

[38]So I advise you to stay away from these men. Leave them alone. If what they are planning is something of their own doing, it will fail. [39]But if God is behind it, you cannot stop it anyway, unless you want to fight against God.

The council members agreed with what he said, [40]and they called the apostles back in. They had them beaten with a whip and warned them not to speak in the name of Jesus. Then they let them go.

[41]The apostles left the council and were happy, because God had considered them worthy to suffer for the sake of Jesus. [42]Every day they spent time in the temple and in one home after another. They never stopped teaching and telling the good news that Jesus is the Messiah.

[a]5.31 *right side:* The place of honor and power.

Prayer Starter: Lord, give me the courage to be your follower, even when it's hard.

Memory Verse: Only Jesus has the power to save! His name is the only one in all the world that can save anyone. —*Acts 4.12*

Stephen

The twelve apostles called the whole group of followers together and said, "We should not give up preaching God's message in order to serve at tables.[a] [3]My friends, choose seven men who are respected and wise and filled with God's Spirit. We will put them in charge of these things. [4]We can spend our time praying and serving God by preaching."

[5]This suggestion pleased everyone, and they began by choosing Stephen. He had great faith and was filled with the Holy Spirit. Then they chose Philip, Prochorus, Nicanor, Timon, Parmenas, and also Nicolaus, who worshiped with the Jewish people[b] in Antioch.

[8]God gave Stephen the power to work great miracles and wonders among the people. [9]But some men from Cyrene and Alexandria were members of a group who called themselves "Free Men."[c] They started arguing with Stephen. Some others from Cilicia and Asia also argued with him. [10]But they were no match for Stephen, who spoke with the great wisdom that the Spirit gave him. [11]So they talked some men into saying, "We heard Stephen say terrible things against Moses and God!"

[12]They turned the people and their leaders and the teachers of the Law of Moses against Stephen. Then they all grabbed Stephen and dragged him in front of the council.

[13]Some men agreed to tell lies about Stephen, and they said, "This man keeps on saying terrible things about this holy temple and the Law of Moses. [14]We have heard him claim that Jesus from Nazareth will destroy this place and change the customs that Moses gave us." [15]Then all the council members stared at Stephen. They saw that his face looked like the face of an angel.

[a]6.2 *to serve at tables:* This may mean either that they were in charge of handing out food to the widows or that they were in charge of the money, since the Greek word "table" may also mean "bank." [b]6.5 *worshiped with the Jewish people:* This translates the Greek word "proselyte" that means a Gentile who had accepted the Jewish religion. [c]6.9 *Free Men:* A group of Jewish men who had once been slaves, but had been freed.

Prayer Starter: Lord, give me faith and wisdom like Stephen's.

Memory Verse: The Lord's followers . . .   *—Acts 8.4*

Stephen Stoned to Death

When the council members heard Stephen's speech, they were angry and furious. ⁵⁵But Stephen was filled with the Holy Spirit. He looked toward heaven, where he saw our glorious God and Jesus standing at his right side.ᵃ ⁵⁶Then Stephen said, "I see heaven open and the Son of Man standing at the right side of God!"

⁵⁷The council members shouted and covered their ears. At once they all attacked Stephen ⁵⁸and dragged him out of the city. Then they started throwing stones at him. The men who had brought charges against him put their coats at the feet of a young man named Saul.ᵇ

⁵⁹As Stephen was being stoned to death, he called out, "Lord Jesus, please welcome me!" ⁶⁰He knelt down and shouted, "Lord, don't blame them for what they have done." Then he died.

8 Saul approved the stoning of Stephen. Some faithful followers of the Lord buried Stephen and mourned very much for him.

At that time the church in Jerusalem suffered terribly. All of the Lord's followers, except the apostles, were scattered everywhere in Judea and Samaria. ³Saul started making a lot of trouble for the church. He went from house to house, arresting men and women and putting them in jail.

⁴The Lord's followers who had been scattered went from place to place, telling the good news. ⁵Philip went to the city of Samaria and told the people about Christ. ⁶They crowded around Philip because they were eager to hear what he was saying and to see him work miracles. ⁷Many people with evil spirits were healed, and the spirits went out of them with a shout. A lot of crippled and lame people were also healed. ⁸Everyone in that city was very glad because of what was happening.

ᵃ7.55 *standing at his right side:* The "right side" is the place of honor and power. "Standing" may mean that Jesus is welcoming Stephen. ᵇ7.58 *Saul:* Better known as Paul, who became a famous follower of Jesus.

Prayer Starter: Lord, as I go from place to place, may I tell the good news.

Memory Verse: The Lord's followers who had been scattered . . .

—Acts 8.4

Simon

For some time a man named Simon had lived in the city of Samaria and had amazed the people. He practiced witchcraft and claimed to be somebody great. ¹⁰Everyone, rich and poor, crowded around him. They said, "This man is the power of God called 'The Great Power.'"

¹¹For a long time, Simon had used witchcraft to amaze the people, and they kept crowding around him. ¹²But when they believed what Philip was saying about God's kingdom and about the name of Jesus Christ, they were all baptized. ¹³Even Simon believed and was baptized. He stayed close to Philip, because he marveled at all the miracles and wonders.

¹⁴The apostles in Jerusalem heard that some people in Samaria had accepted God's message, and they sent Peter and John. ¹⁵When the two apostles arrived, they prayed that the people would be given the Holy Spirit. ¹⁶Before this, the Holy Spirit had not been given to anyone in Samaria, though some of them had been baptized in the name of the Lord Jesus. ¹⁷Peter and John then placed their hands on everyone who had faith in the Lord, and they were given the Holy Spirit.

¹⁸Simon noticed that the Spirit was given only when the apostles placed their hands on the people. So he brought money ¹⁹and said to Peter and John, "Let me have this power too! Then anyone I place my hands on will also be given the Holy Spirit."

²⁰Peter said to him, "You and your money will both end up in hell if you think you can buy God's gift! ²¹You don't have any part in this, and God sees that your heart isn't right. ²²Get rid of these evil thoughts and ask God to forgive you.

Prayer Starter: Lord, keep me from loving money too much.

Memory Verse: The Lord's followers who had been scattered went from place to place . . .   —*Acts 8.4*

Philip and the Ethiopian

The Lord's angel said to Philip, "Go south[a] along the desert road that leads from Jerusalem to Gaza."[b] [27]So Philip left.

An important Ethiopian official happened to be going along that road in his chariot. He was the chief treasurer for Candace, the Queen of Ethiopia. The official had gone to Jerusalem to worship [28]and was now on his way home. He was sitting in his chariot, reading the book of the prophet Isaiah.

[29]The Spirit told Philip to catch up with the chariot. [30]Philip ran up close and heard the man reading aloud from the book of Isaiah. Philip asked him, "Do you understand what you are reading?"

[31]The official answered, "How can I understand unless someone helps me?" He then invited Philip to come up and sit beside him.

[32]The man was reading the passage that said,

"He was led like a sheep on its way to be killed.
He was silent as a lamb whose wool is being cut off,
    and he did not say a word.
[33] He was treated like a nobody
    and did not receive a fair trial.
How can he have children,
    if his life is snatched away?"

[34]The official said to Philip, "Tell me, was the prophet talking about himself or about someone else?" [35]So Philip began at this place in the Scriptures and explained the good news about Jesus.

[a]8.26 *Go south:* Or "About noon go." [b]8.26 *the desert road that leads from Jerusalem to Gaza:* Or "the road that leads from Jerusalem to Gaza in the desert."

Prayer Starter: Lord, bless all your preachers, teachers, and evangelists who are explaining the good news about Jesus.

Memory Verse: The Lord's followers who had been scattered went from place to place, telling . . .
      —*Acts 8.4*

Saul Meets Jesus

Saul kept on threatening to kill the Lord's followers. He even went to the high priest ²and asked for letters to their leaders in Damascus. He did this because he wanted to arrest and take to Jerusalem any man or woman who had accepted the Lord's Way.ᵃ ³When Saul had almost reached Damascus, a bright light from heaven suddenly flashed around him. ⁴He fell to the ground and heard a voice that said, "Saul! Saul! Why are you so cruel to me?"

5"Who are you?" Saul asked.

"I am Jesus," the Lord answered. "I am the one you are so cruel to. 6Now get up and go into the city, where you will be told what to do."

7The men with Saul stood there speechless. They had heard the voice, but they had not seen anyone. 8Saul got up from the ground, and when he opened his eyes, he could not see a thing. Someone then led him by the hand to Damascus, 9and for three days he was blind and did not eat or drink.

10A follower named Ananias lived in Damascus, and the Lord spoke to him in a vision. Ananias answered, "Lord, here I am."

11The Lord said to him, "Get up and go to the house of Judas on Straight Street. When you get there, you will find a man named Saul from the city of Tarsus. Saul is praying, 12and he has seen a vision. He saw a man named Ananias coming to him and putting his hands on him, so that he could see again."

13Ananias replied: "Lord, a lot of people have told me about the terrible things this man has done to your followers in Jerusalem. 14Now the chief priests have given him the power to come here and arrest anyone who worships in your name."

15The Lord said to Ananias, "Go! I have chosen him to tell foreigners, kings, and the people of Israel about me. 16I will show him how much he must suffer for worshiping in my name."

17Ananias left and went into the house where Saul was staying. Ananias placed his hands on him and said, "Saul, the Lord Jesus has sent me. He is the same one who appeared to you along the road. He wants you to be able to see and to be filled with the Holy Spirit."

18Suddenly something like fish scales fell from Saul's eyes, and he could see. He got up and was baptized.

a9.2 *accepted the Lord's Way:* In the book of Acts, this means to become a follower of the Lord Jesus.

Prayer Starter: May my friends who don't know Christ come to love and trust him, just as Saul did.

Memory Verse: The Lord's followers who had been scattered went from place to place, telling the good news.   —*Acts 8.4*

Saul Escapes
Damascus

For several days Saul stayed with the Lord's followers in Damascus. [20]Soon he went to the Jewish meeting places and started telling people that Jesus is the Son of God. [21]Everyone who heard Saul was amazed and said, "Isn't this the man who caused so much trouble for those people in Jerusalem who worship in the name of Jesus? Didn't he come here to arrest them and take them to the chief priests?"

[22]Saul preached with such power that he completely confused the Jewish people in Damascus, as he tried to show them that Jesus is the Messiah.

[23]Later some of them made plans to kill Saul, [24]but he found out about it. He learned that they were guarding the gates of the city day and night in order to kill him. [25]Then one night his followers let him down over the city wall in a large basket.

[26]When Saul arrived in Jerusalem, he tried to join the followers. But they were all afraid of him, because they did not believe he was a true follower. [27]Then Barnabas helped him by taking him to the apostles. He explained how Saul had seen the Lord and how the Lord had spoken to him. Barnabas also said that when Saul was in Damascus, he had spoken bravely in the name of Jesus.

[28]Saul moved about freely with the followers in Jerusalem and told everyone about the Lord. [29]He was always arguing with the Jews who spoke Greek, and so they tried to kill him. [30]But the followers found out about this and took Saul to Caesarea. From there they sent him to the city of Tarsus.

[31]The church in Judea, Galilee, and Samaria now had a time of peace and kept on worshiping the Lord. The church became stronger, as the Holy Spirit encouraged it and helped it grow.

Prayer Starter: Help me to speak bravely in the name of the Lord.

Memory Verse: God is pleased . . .   *—Acts 10.35*

Dorcas

While Peter was traveling from place to place, he visited the Lord's followers who lived in the town of Lydda. ³³There he met a man named Aeneas, who for eight years had been sick in bed and could not move. ³⁴Peter said to Aeneas, "Jesus Christ has healed you! Get up and make your bed."ᵃ Right away he stood up.

³⁵Many people in the towns of Lydda and Sharon saw Aeneas and became followers of the Lord.

³⁶In Joppa there was a follower named Tabitha. Her Greek name was Dorcas, which means "deer." She was always doing good things for people and had given much to the poor. ³⁷But she got sick and died, and her body was washed and placed in an upstairs room. ³⁸Joppa wasn't far from Lydda, and the followers heard that Peter was there. They sent two men to say to him, "Please come with us as quickly as you can!" ³⁹Right away, Peter went with them.

The men took Peter upstairs into the room. Many widows were there crying. They showed him the coats and clothes that Dorcas had made while she was still alive.

⁴⁰After Peter had sent everyone out of the room, he knelt down and prayed. Then he turned to the body of Dorcas and said, "Tabitha, get up!" The woman opened her eyes, and when she saw Peter, she sat up. ⁴¹He took her by the hand and helped her to her feet.

Peter called in the widows and the other followers and showed them that Dorcas had been raised from death. ⁴²Everyone in Joppa heard what had happened, and many of them put their faith in the Lord. ⁴³Peter stayed on for a while in Joppa in the house of a man named Simon, who made leather.

ª9.34 *and make up your bed:* Or "and fix something to eat."

Prayer Starter: I love to read your Bible each day, Lord. Thank you for stories like this one.

Memory Verse: God is pleased with everyone who worships him . . .
—*Acts 10.35*

| Peter's |
| Chains |
| Fall Off |

At that time King Herod[a] caused terrible suffering for some members of the church. [2]He ordered soldiers to cut off the head of James, the brother of John. [3]When Herod saw that this pleased the Jewish people, he had Peter arrested during the Festival of Thin Bread. [4]He put Peter in jail and ordered four squads of soldiers to guard him. Herod planned to put him on trial in public after the festival.

[5]While Peter was being kept in jail, the church never stopped praying to God for him.

[6]The night before Peter was to be put on trial, he was asleep and bound by two chains. A soldier was guarding him on each side, and two other soldiers were guarding the entrance to the jail. [7]Suddenly an angel from the Lord appeared, and light flashed around in the cell. The angel poked Peter in the side and woke him up. Then he said, "Quick! Get up!"

The chains fell off his hands, [8]and the angel said, "Get dressed and put on your sandals." Peter did what he was told. Then the angel said, "Now put on your coat and follow me." [9]Peter left with the angel, but he thought everything was only a dream. [10]They went past the two groups of soldiers, and when they came to the iron gate to the city, it opened by itself. They went out and were going along the street, when all at once the angel disappeared.

[11]Peter now realized what had happened, and he said, "I am certain that the Lord sent his angel to rescue me from Herod and from everything the Jewish leaders planned to do to me." [12]Then Peter went to the house of Mary the mother of John whose other name was Mark. Many of the Lord's followers had come together there and were praying.

[13]Peter knocked on the gate, and a servant named Rhoda came to answer. [14]When she heard Peter's voice, she was too excited to open the gate. She ran back into the house and said that Peter was standing there.

[15]"You are crazy!" everyone told her. But she kept saying that it was Peter. Then they said, "It must be his angel."[b] [16]But Peter kept on knocking, until finally they opened the gate. They saw him and were completely amazed.

[17]Peter motioned for them to keep quiet. Then he told how the Lord had led him out of jail. He also said, "Tell James[c] and the others what has happened." After that, he left and went somewhere else.

[18]The next morning the soldiers who had been on guard were terribly worried and wondered what had happened to Peter. [19]Herod ordered his

own soldiers to search for him, but they could not find him. Then he questioned the guards and had them put to death. After this, Herod left Judea to stay in Caesarea for a while.

ᵃ12.1 *Herod:* Herod Agrippa I, the grandson of Herod the Great. ᵇ12.15 *his angel:* Probably meaning "his guardian angel." ᶜ12.17 *James:* The brother of the Lord.

Prayer Starter: Send your angels to watch over us, Lord, just as they cared for Peter.

Memory Verse: God is pleased with everyone who worships him and does right . . .
—*Acts 10.35*

Elymas, Son of the Devil

The church at Antioch had several prophets and teachers. They were Barnabas, Simeon, also called Niger, Lucius from Cyrene, Manaen, who was Herod's[a] close friend, and Saul. [2]While they were worshiping the Lord and going without eating,[b] the Holy Spirit told them, "Appoint Barnabas and Saul to do the work for which I have chosen them." [3]Everyone prayed and went without eating for a while longer. Next, they placed their hands on Barnabas and Saul to show that they had been appointed to do this work. Then everyone sent them on their way.

[4]After Barnabas and Saul had been sent by the Holy Spirit, they went to Seleucia. From there they sailed to the island of Cyprus. [5]They arrived at Salamis and began to preach God's message in the Jewish meeting places. They also had John[c] as a helper.

[6]Barnabas and Saul went all the way to the city of Paphos on the other end of the island, where they met a Jewish man named Bar-Jesus. He practiced witchcraft and was a false prophet. [7]He also worked for Sergius Paulus, who was very smart and was the governor of the island. Sergius Paulus wanted to hear God's message, and he sent for Barnabas and Saul. [8]But Bar-Jesus, whose other name was Elymas, was against them. He even tried to keep the governor from having faith in the Lord.

[9]Then Saul, better known as Paul, was filled with the Holy Spirit. He looked straight at Elymas [10]and said, "You son of the devil! You are a liar, a crook, and an enemy of everything that is right. When will you stop speaking against the true ways of the Lord? [11]The Lord is going to punish you by making you completely blind for a while."

Suddenly the man's eyes were covered by a dark mist, and he went around trying to get someone to lead him by the hand. [12]When the governor saw what had happened, he was amazed at this teaching about the Lord. So he put his faith in the Lord.

[a]13.1 *Herod's:* Herod Antipas, the son of Herod the Great. [b]13.2 *going without eating:* The Jews often went without eating as a way of showing how much they loved God. This is also called "fasting." [c]13.5 *John:* Whose other name was Mark.

Prayer Starter: Thank you for my eyes, ears, nose, and mouth.

Memory Verse: God is pleased with everyone who worships him and does right, no matter what nation . . .
—*Acts 10.35*

> ### Paul and Barnabas Preach

When David was alive, he obeyed God. Then after he died, he was buried in the family grave, and his body decayed. [37]But God raised Jesus from death, and his body did not decay.

[38]My friends, the message is that Jesus can forgive your sins! The Law of Moses could not set you free from all your sins. [39]But everyone who has faith in Jesus is set free. [40]Make sure that what the prophets have said doesn't happen to you. They said,

[41] "Look, you people who make fun of God!
    Be amazed and disappear.
I will do something today that you won't believe,
    even if someone tells you about it!"

[42]As Paul and Barnabas were leaving the meeting, the people begged them to say more about these same things on the next Sabbath. [43]After the service, many Jews and a lot of Gentiles who worshiped God went with them. Paul and Barnabas begged them all to remain faithful to God, who had been so kind to them.

[44]The next Sabbath almost everyone in town came to hear the message about the Lord.[a] [45]When the Jewish people saw the crowds, they were very jealous. They insulted Paul and spoke against everything he said.

[46]But Paul and Barnabas bravely said:

We had to tell God's message to you before we told it to anyone else. But you rejected the message! This proves that you don't deserve eternal life. Now we are going to the Gentiles. [47]The Lord has given us this command,

"I have placed you here as a light for the Gentiles.
You are to take the saving power of God
    to people everywhere on earth."

[48]This message made the Gentiles glad, and they praised what they had heard about the Lord.[b] Everyone who had been chosen for eternal life then put their faith in the Lord.

[49]The message about the Lord spread all over the region.

---

[a]13.44 *the Lord:* Some manuscripts have "God." [b]13.48 *the Lord:* Some manuscripts have "God."

Prayer Starter: I want to trust you, Lord, when things seem to be going badly.

Memory Verse: God is pleased with everyone who worships him and does right, no matter what nation they come from. —*Acts 10.35*

The Stoning of Paul

In Lystra there was a man who had been born with crippled feet and had never been able to walk. ⁹The man was listening to Paul speak, when Paul saw that he had faith in Jesus and could be healed. So he looked straight at the man ¹⁰and shouted, "Stand up!" The man jumped up and started walking around.

¹¹When the crowd saw what Paul had done, they yelled out in the language of Lycaonia, "The gods have turned into humans and have come down to us!" ¹²The people then gave Barnabas the name Zeus, and they gave Paul the name Hermes,ᵃ because he did the talking.

¹³The temple of Zeus was near the entrance to the city. Its priest and the crowds wanted to offer a sacrifice to Barnabas and Paul. So the priest brought some bulls and flowers to the city gates. ¹⁴When the two apostles found out about this, they tore their clothes in horror and ran to the crowd, shouting:

¹⁵Why are you doing this? We are humans just like you. Please give up all this foolishness. Turn to the living God, who made the sky, the earth, the sea, and everything in them. ¹⁶In times past, God let each nation go its own way. ¹⁷But he showed that he was there by the good things he did. God sends rain from heaven and makes your crops grow. He gives food to you and makes your hearts glad.

¹⁸Even after Paul and Barnabas had said all this, they could hardly keep the people from offering a sacrifice to them.

¹⁹Some Jewish leaders from Antioch and Iconium came and turned the crowds against Paul. They hit him with stones and dragged him out of the city, thinking he was dead. ²⁰But when the Lord's followers gathered around Paul, he stood up and went back into the city. The next day he and Barnabas went to Derbe.

ᵃ14.12 *Hermes:* The Greeks thought of Hermes as the messenger of the other gods, especially of Zeus, their chief god.

Prayer Starter: Thank you for giving us food and making our hearts glad.

Memory Verse: Stop all your dirty talk. . . .　　　*—Ephesians 4.29*

The Jerusalem Meeting

Some people came from Judea and started teaching the Lord's followers that they could not be saved, unless they were circumcised as Moses had taught. ²This caused trouble, and Paul and Barnabas argued with them about this teaching. So it was decided to send Paul and Barnabas and a few others to Jerusalem to discuss this problem with the apostles and the church leaders.

³The men who were sent by the church went through Phoenicia and Samaria, telling how the Gentiles had turned to God. This news made the Lord's followers very happy. ⁴When the men arrived in Jerusalem, they were welcomed by the church, including the apostles and the leaders. They told them everything God had helped them do. ⁵But some Phar-

isees had become followers of the Lord. They stood up and said, "Gentiles who have faith in the Lord must be circumcised and told to obey the Law of Moses."

⁶The apostles and church leaders met to discuss this problem about Gentiles. ⁷They had talked it over for a long time, when Peter got up and said:

My friends, you know that God decided long ago to let me be the one from your group to preach the good news to the Gentiles. God did this so that they would hear and obey him. [8]He knows what is in everyone's heart. And he showed that he had chosen the Gentiles, when he gave them the Holy Spirit, just as he had given his Spirit to us. [9]God treated them in the same way that he treated us. They put their faith in him, and he made their hearts pure.

[10]Now why are you trying to make God angry by placing a heavy burden on these followers? This burden was too heavy for us or our ancestors. [11]But our Lord Jesus was kind to us, and we are saved by faith in him, just as the Gentiles are.

[12]Everyone kept quiet and listened as Barnabas and Paul told how God had given them the power to work a lot of miracles and wonders for the Gentiles.

Prayer Starter: Thank you for your church, dear Lord.

Memory Verse: Stop all your dirty talk. Say the right thing . . .
—*Ephesians 4.29*

The Apostles' Letter

The apostles, the leaders, and all the church members decided to send some men to Antioch along with Paul and Barnabas. They chose Silas and Judas Barsabbas,[a] who were two leaders of the Lord's followers. [23]They wrote a letter that said:

We apostles and leaders send friendly greetings to all of you Gentiles who are followers of the Lord in Antioch, Syria, and Cilicia.

[24]We have heard that some people from here have terribly upset you by what they said. But we did not send them! [25]So we met together and decided to choose some men and to send them to you along with our good friends Barnabas and Paul. [26]These men have risked their lives for our Lord Jesus Christ. [27]We are also sending Judas and Silas, who will tell you in person the same things that we are writing.

[28]The Holy Spirit has shown us that we should not place any extra burden on you. [29]But you should not eat anything offered to idols. You should not eat any meat that still has the blood in it or any meat of any animal that has been strangled. You must also not commit any terrible sexual sins. If you follow these instructions, you will do well.

We send our best wishes.

[30]The four men left Jerusalem and went to Antioch. Then they called the church members together and gave them the letter. [31]When the letter was read, everyone was pleased and greatly encouraged.

[a]15.22 *Judas Barsabbas:* He may have been a brother of Joseph Barsabbas, but the name "Barsabbas" was often used by the Jewish people.

Prayer Starter: Bless those, O Lord, who have gone to other nations, taking the message of Jesus.

Memory Verse: Stop all your dirty talk. Say the right thing at the right time . . .
                                                          —*Ephesians 4.29*

Paul's Travels

Paul and Silas went back to Derbe and Lystra, where there was a follower named Timothy. His mother was also a follower. She was Jewish, and his father was Greek. [2]The Lord's followers in Lystra and Iconium said good things about Timothy, [3]and Paul wanted him to go with them. But Paul first had him circumcised, because all the Jewish people around there knew that Timothy's father was Greek.[a]

[4]As Paul and the others went from city to city, they told the followers what the apostles and leaders in Jerusalem had decided, and they urged them to follow these instructions. [5]The churches became stronger in their faith, and each day more people put their faith in the Lord.

[6]Paul and his friends went through Phrygia and Galatia, but the Holy Spirit would not let them preach in Asia. [7]After they arrived in Mysia, they tried to go into Bithynia, but the Spirit of Jesus would not let them. [8]So they went on through[b] Mysia until they came to Troas.

[9]During the night, Paul had a vision of someone from Macedonia who was standing there begging him, "Come over to Macedonia and help us!" [10]After Paul had seen the vision, we began looking for a way to go to Macedonia. We were sure that God had called us to preach the good news there.

[a]16.3 *had him circumcised . . . Timothy's father was Greek:* Timothy would not have been acceptable to the Jews unless he had been circumcised, and Greeks did not circumcise their sons. [b]16.8 *went on through:* Or "passed by."

Prayer Starter: Lead me day by day, dear Lord, just as you led the apostle Paul.

Memory Verse: Stop all your dirty talk. Say the right thing at the right time and help others . . .   —*Ephesians 4.29*

Followers in Philippi

W e sailed straight from Troas to Samothrace, and the next day we arrived in Neapolis. ¹²From there we went to Philippi, which is a Roman colony in the first district of Macedonia.ᵃ

We spent several days in Philippi. ¹³Then on the Sabbath we went outside the city gate to a place by the river, where we thought there would be a Jewish meeting place for prayer. We sat down and talked with the women who came. ¹⁴One of them was Lydia, who was from the city of Thyatira and sold expensive purple cloth. She was a worshiper of the Lord God, and he made her willing to accept what Paul was saying. ¹⁵Then after she and her family were baptized, she kept on begging us, "If you think I really do have faith in the Lord, come stay in my home." Finally, we accepted her invitation.

ᵃ16.12 *in the first district of Macedonia:* Some manuscripts have "and the leading city of Macedonia."

Prayer Starter: Teach me to pray each day, to talk to you friend-to-friend.

Memory Verse: Stop all your dirty talk. Say the right thing at the right time and help others by what you say. —*Ephesians 4.29*

Paul and Silas Are Jailed

The crowd joined in the attack on Paul and Silas. Then the officials tore the clothes off the two men and ordered them to be beaten with a whip. [23]After they had been badly beaten, they were put in jail, and the jailer was told to guard them carefully. [24]The jailer did as he was told. He put them deep inside the jail and chained their feet to heavy blocks of wood.

[25]About midnight Paul and Silas were praying and singing praises to God, while the other prisoners listened. [26]Suddenly a strong earthquake shook the jail to its foundations. The doors opened, and the chains fell from all the prisoners.

[27]When the jailer woke up and saw that the doors were open, he thought that the prisoners had escaped. He pulled out his sword and was about to kill himself. [28]But Paul shouted, "Don't harm yourself! No one has escaped."

[29]The jailer asked for a torch and went into the jail. He was shaking all over as he knelt down in front of Paul and Silas. [30]After he had led them out of the jail, he asked, "What must I do to be saved?"

[31]They replied, "Have faith in the Lord Jesus and you will be saved! This is also true for everyone who lives in your home."

[32]Then Paul and Silas told him and everyone else in his house about the Lord. [33]While it was still night, the jailer took them to a place where he could wash their cuts and bruises. Then he and everyone in his home were baptized. [34]They were very glad that they had put their faith in God. After this, the jailer took Paul and Silas to his home and gave them something to eat.

Prayer Starter: Be with those in the jails and prisons, Lord, and give them the hope of the Lord Jesus.

Memory Verse: They replied . . .   —*Acts 16.31a*

<table>
<tr><td>

**Paul's
Sermon
in Athens**

</td><td>

While Paul was waiting in Athens, he was upset to see all the idols in the city. [17]He went to the Jewish meeting place to speak to the Jews and to anyone who worshiped with them. Day after day he also spoke to everyone he met in the market. [18]Some of them were Epicureans[a] and some were Stoics,[b] and they started arguing with him.

</td></tr>
</table>

People were asking, "What is this know-it-all trying to say?"

Some even said, "Paul must be preaching about foreign gods! That's what he means when he talks about Jesus and about people rising from death."[c]

[19]They brought Paul before a council called the Areopagus, and said, "Tell us what your new teaching is all about. [20]We have heard you say some strange things, and we want to know what you mean."

[21]More than anything else the people of Athens and the foreigners living there loved to hear and to talk about anything new. [22]So Paul stood up in front of the council and said:

People of Athens, I see that you are very religious. [23]As I was going through your city and looking at the things you worship, I found an altar with the words, "To an Unknown God." You worship this God, but you don't really know him. So I want to tell you about him. [24]This God made the world and everything in it. He is Lord of heaven and earth, and he doesn't live in temples built by human hands. [25]He doesn't need help from anyone. He gives life, breath, and everything else to all people. [26]From one person God made all nations who live on earth, and he decided when and where every nation would be.

[a]17.18 *Epicureans:* People who followed the teaching of a man named Epicurus, who taught that happiness should be the main goal in life. [b]17.18 *Stoics:* Followers of a man named Zeno, who taught that people should learn self-control and be guided by their consciences. [c]17.18 *people rising from death:* Or "a goddess named 'Rising from Death.'"

Prayer Starter: Show me those I can invite to church and tell about you.

Memory Verse: They replied, "Have faith . . ."   —*Acts 16.31a*

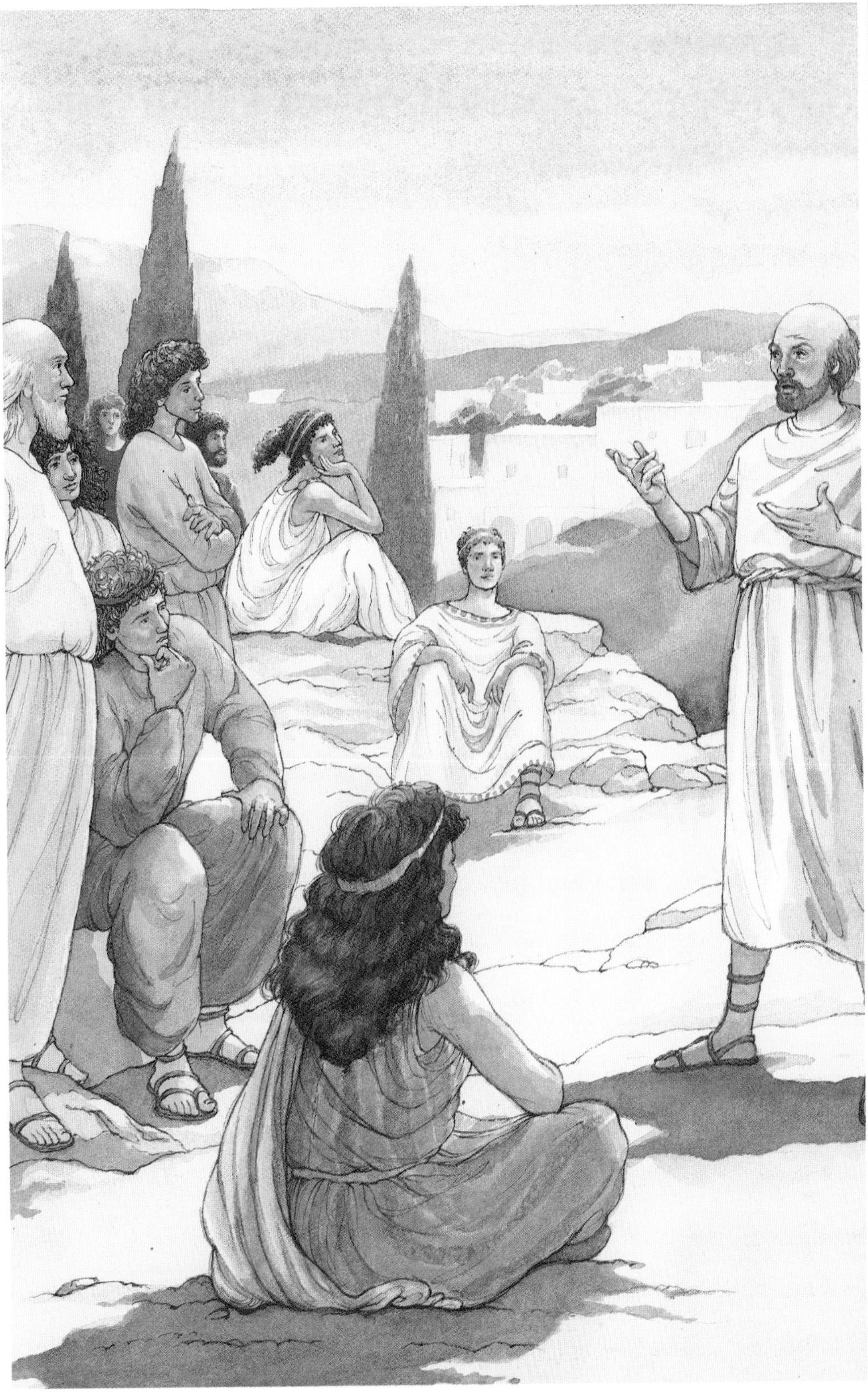

Paul, the Tent Maker

Paul left Athens and went to Corinth, ²where he met Aquila, a Jewish man from Pontus. Not long before this, Aquila had come from Italy with his wife Priscilla, because Emperor Claudius had ordered the Jewish people to leave Rome.ᵃ Paul went to see Aquila and Priscilla ³and found out that they were tent makers. Paul was a tent maker too. So he stayed with them, and they worked together.

⁴Every Sabbath, Paul went to the Jewish meeting place. He spoke to Jews and Gentilesᵇ and tried to win them over. ⁵But after Silas and Timothy came from Macedonia, he spent all his time preaching to the Jews about Jesus the Messiah. ⁶Finally, they turned against him and insulted him. So he shook the dust from his clothesᶜ and told them, "Whatever happens to you will be your own fault! I am not to blame. From now on I am going to preach to the Gentiles."

⁷Paul then moved into the house of a man named Titius Justus, who worshiped God and lived next door to the meeting place. ⁸Crispus was the leader of the meeting place. He and everyone in his family put their faith in the Lord. Many others in Corinth also heard the message, and all the people who had faith in the Lord were baptized.

ᵃ18.2 *Emperor Claudius had ordered the Jewish people to leave Rome:* Probably A.D. 49, though it may have been A.D. 41. ᵇ18.4 *Gentiles:* Here the word is "Greeks." ᶜ18.6 *shook the dust from his clothes:* This means the same as shaking dust from the feet.

Prayer Starter: Give me good friends, Lord, who will help me be stronger.

Memory Verse: They replied, "Have faith in the Lord Jesus . . ."
—*Acts 16.31a*

Jesus Appears in a Vision

Oₙe night, Paul had a vision, and in it the Lord said, "Don't be afraid to keep on preaching. Don't stop! ¹⁰I am with you, and you won't be harmed. Many people in this city belong to me." ¹¹Paul stayed on in Corinth for a year and a half, teaching God's message to the people.

¹²While Gallio was governor of Achaia, some of the Jewish leaders got together and grabbed Paul. They brought him into court ¹³and said, "This man is trying to make our people worship God in a way that is against our Law!"

¹⁴Even before Paul could speak, Gallio said, "If you were charging this man with a crime or some other wrong, I would have to listen to you. ¹⁵But since this concerns only words, names, and your own law, you will have to take care of it. I refuse to judge such matters." ¹⁶Then he sent them out of the court. ¹⁷The crowd grabbed Sosthenes, the Jewish leader, and beat him up in front of the court. But none of this mattered to Gallio.

¹⁸After Paul had stayed for a while with the Lord's followers in Corinth, he told them good-by and sailed on to Syria with Aquila and Priscilla. But before he left, he had his head shaved[a] at Cenchreae because he had made a promise to God.

[a]18.18 *he had his head shaved:* Paul had promised to be a "Nazirite" for a while. This meant that for the time of the promise, he could not cut his hair or drink wine. When the time was over, he would have to cut his hair and offer a sacrifice to God.

Prayer Starter: Give strength to Christians around the world who are being mistreated because of their faith in you, O Lord.

Memory Verse: They replied, "Have faith in the Lord Jesus and you . . ."

　　　　　　　　　　　　　　　　　　　　　　　—*Acts 16.31a*

Priscilla, Aquila, and Apollos

The three of them arrived in Ephesus, where Paul left Priscilla and Aquila. He then went into the Jewish meeting place to talk with the people there. [20]They asked him to stay longer, but he refused. [21]He told them good-by and said, "If God lets me, I will come back."

[22]Paul sailed to Caesarea, where he greeted the church. Then he went on to Antioch. [23]After staying there for a while, he left and visited several places in Galatia and Phyrgia. He helped the followers there to become stronger in their faith.

[24]A Jewish man named Apollos came to Ephesus. Apollos had been born in the city of Alexandria. He was a very good speaker and knew a lot about the Scriptures. [25]He also knew much about the Lord's Way,[a] and he spoke about it with great excitement. What he taught about Jesus was right, but all he knew was John's message about baptism.

[26]Apollos started speaking bravely in the Jewish meeting place. But when Priscilla and Aquila heard him, they took him to their home and helped him understand God's Way even better.

[27]Apollos decided to travel through Achaia. So the Lord's followers wrote letters, encouraging the followers there to welcome him. After Apollos arrived in Achaia, he was a great help to

everyone who had put their faith in the Lord Jesus because of God's kindness. [28]He got into fierce arguments with the Jewish people, and in public he used the Scriptures to prove that Jesus is the Messiah.

19 While Apollos was in Corinth, Paul traveled across the hill country to Ephesus, where he met some of the Lord's followers. [2]He asked them, "When you put your faith in Jesus, were you given the Holy Spirit?"

"No!" they answered. "We have never even heard of the Holy Spirit."

[3]"Then why were you baptized?" Paul asked.

They answered, "Because of what John taught."[b]

[4]Paul replied, "John baptized people so that they would turn to God. But he also told them that someone else was coming, and that they should put their faith in him. Jesus is the one that John was talking about." [5]After the people heard Paul say this, they were baptized in the name of the Lord Jesus.

[a]18.25 *the Lord's Way:* In the book of Acts, this means to become a follower of the Lord Jesus.
[b]19.3 *Then why were you baptized? . . . Because of what John taught:* Or "In whose name were you baptized? . . . We were baptized in John's name."

Prayer Starter: You are so kind, dear Lord. Give me a kind heart, too.

Memory Verse: They replied, "Have faith in the Lord Jesus and you will be saved!"
—*Acts 16.31a*

The Sons of Sceva

G od gave Paul the power to work great miracles. [12]People even took handkerchiefs and aprons that had touched Paul's body, and they carried them to everyone who was sick. All of the sick people were healed, and the evil spirits went out.

[13]Some Jewish men started going around trying to force out evil spirits by using the name of the Lord Jesus. They said to the spirits, "Come out in the name of that same Jesus that Paul preaches about!"

[14]Seven sons of a Jewish high priest named Sceva were doing this, [15]when an evil spirit said to them, "I know Jesus! And I have heard about Paul. But who are you?" [16]Then the man with the evil spirit jumped on them and beat them up. They ran out of the house, naked and bruised.

[17]When all the Jews and Gentiles[a] in Ephesus heard about this, they were so frightened that they praised the name of the Lord Jesus. [18]Many who were followers now started telling everyone about the evil things they had been doing. [19]Some who had been practicing witchcraft even brought their books and burned them in public. These books were worth about fifty thousand silver coins. [20]So the Lord's message spread and became even more powerful.

[a]19.17 *Gentiles:* The text has "Greeks," which probably means people who were not Jews. But it may mean Gentiles who worshiped with Jews.

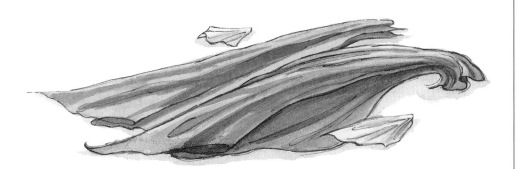

Prayer Starter: Lord, thank you that I can know *you* and not just know *about* you.

Memory Verse: Remember . . .   *—Acts 20.35b*

Riot at Ephesus

After all of this had happened, Paul decided[a] to visit Macedonia and Achaia on his way to Jerusalem. Paul had said, "From there I will go on to Rome." ²²So he sent his two helpers, Timothy and Erastus, to Macedonia. But he stayed on in Asia for a while.

²³At that time there was serious trouble because of the Lord's Way.[b] ²⁴A silversmith named Demetrius had a business that made silver models of the temple of the goddess Artemis. Those who worked for him earned a lot of money. ²⁵Demetrius brought together everyone who was in the same business and said:

Friends, you know that we make a good living at this. ²⁶But you have surely seen and heard how this man Paul is upsetting a lot of people, not only in Ephesus, but almost everywhere in Asia. He claims that the gods we humans make are not really gods at all. ²⁷Everyone will start saying terrible things about our business. They will stop respecting the temple of the goddess Artemis, who is worshiped in Asia and all over the world. Our great goddess will be forgotten!

²⁸When the workers heard this, they got angry and started shouting, "Great is Artemis, the goddess of the Ephesians!" ²⁹Soon the whole city was in a riot, and some men grabbed Gaius and Aristarchus, who had come from Macedonia with Paul. Then everyone in the crowd rushed to the place where the town meetings were held.

³⁰Paul wanted to go out and speak to the people, but the Lord's followers would not let him. ³¹A few of the local officials were friendly to Paul, and they sent someone to warn him not to go.

[a]19.21 *Paul decided:* Or "Paul was led by the Holy Spirit." [b]19.23 *the Lord's Way:* In the book of Acts, this means to become a follower of the Lord Jesus.

Prayer Starter: Comfort and encourage me today, heavenly Father.

Memory Verse: Remember that our Lord Jesus said . . . —*Acts 20.35b*

When the riot was over, Paul sent for the followers and encouraged them. He then told them good-by and left for Macedonia. [2]As he traveled from place to place, he encouraged the followers with many messages. Finally, he went to Greece[a] [3]and stayed there for three months.

Paul was about to sail to Syria. But some of the Jewish leaders plotted against him, so he decided to return by way of Macedonia. [4]With him were Sopater, son of Pyrrhus from Berea, and

Aristarchus and Secundus from Thessalonica. Gaius from Derbe was also with him, and so were Timothy and the two Asians, Tychicus and Trophimus. [5]They went on ahead to Troas and waited for us there. [6]After the Festival of Thin Bread, we sailed from Philippi. Five days later we met them in Troas and stayed there for a week.

[7]On the first day of the week[b] we met to break bread together.[c] Paul spoke to the people until midnight because he was leaving the next morning. [8]In the upstairs room where we were meeting, there were a lot of lamps. [9]A young man by the name of Eutychus was sitting on a window sill. While Paul was speaking, the young man got very sleepy. Finally, he went to sleep and fell three floors all the way down to the ground. When they picked him up, he was dead.

[10]Paul went down and bent over Eutychus. He took him in his arms and said, "Don't worry! He's alive." [11]After Paul had gone back upstairs, he broke bread, and ate with us. He then spoke until dawn and left. [12]Then the followers took the young man home alive and were very happy.

[13]Paul decided to travel by land to Assos. The rest of us went on

ahead by ship, and we were to take him aboard there. [14]When he met us in Assos, he came aboard, and we sailed on to Mitylene. [15]The next day we came to a place near Chios, and the following day we reached Samos. The day after that we sailed to Miletus. [16]Paul had decided to sail on past Ephesus, because he did not want to spend too much time in Asia. He was in a hurry and wanted to be in Jerusalem in time for Pentecost.[d]

[a]20.2 *Greece:* Probably Corinth. [b]20.7 *On the first day of the week:* Since the Jewish day began at sunset, the meeting would have begun in the evening. [c]20.7 *break bread together:* They ate together and celebrated the Lord's Supper. [d]20.16 *in time for Pentecost:* The Jewish people liked to be in Jerusalem for this festival.

Prayer Starter: God, bless me when I'm at church. May I stay awake and alert as I worship you and learn more about you there.

Memory Verse: Remember that our Lord Jesus said, "More blessings . . ."
—*Acts 20.35b*

Church Leaders from Ephesus

From Miletus, Paul sent a message for the church leaders at Ephesus to come and meet with him. ¹⁸When they got there, he said:

You know everything I did during the time I was with you when I first came to Asia. ¹⁹Some of the Jews plotted against me and caused me a lot of sorrow and trouble. But I served the Lord and was humble. ²⁰When I preached in public or taught in your homes, I didn't hold back from telling anything that would help you. ²¹I told Jews and Gentiles to turn to God and have faith in our Lord Jesus.

²²I don't know what will happen to me in Jerusalem, but I must obey God's Spirit and go there. ²³In every city I visit, I am told by the Holy Spirit that I will be put in jail and will be in trouble in Jerusalem. ²⁴But I don't care what happens to me, as long as I finish the work that the Lord Jesus gave me to do. And that work is to tell the good news about God's great kindness.

[25]I have gone from place to place, preaching to you about God's kingdom, but now I know that none of you will ever see me again. [26]I tell you today that I am no longer responsible for any of you! [27]I have told you everything God wants you to know. [28]Look after yourselves and everyone the Holy Spirit has placed in your care. Be like shepherds to God's church. It is the flock that he bought with the blood of his own Son.[a]

[29]I know that after I am gone, others will come like fierce wolves to attack you. [30]Some of your own people will tell lies to win over the Lord's followers. [31]Be on your guard! Remember how day and night for three years I kept warning you with tears in my eyes.

[32]I now place you in God's care. Remember the message about his great kindness! This message can help you and give you what belongs to you as God's people. [33]I have never wanted anyone's money or clothes. [34]You know how I have worked with my own hands to make a living for myself and my friends. [35]By everything I did, I showed how you should work to help everyone who is weak. Remember that our Lord Jesus said, "More blessings come from giving than from receiving."

[36]After Paul had finished speaking, he knelt down with all of them and prayed. [37]Everyone cried and hugged and kissed him. [38]They were especially sad because Paul had told them, "You will never see me again."

Then they went with him to the ship.

---

[a]20.28 *the blood of his own Son:* Or "his own blood."

Prayer Starter: Help me remember that more blessings come from giving than receiving.

Memory Verse: Remember that our Lord Jesus said, "More blessings come from giving . . ."   —*Acts 20.35b*

Paul's Many
Travels

After saying good-by, we sailed straight to Cos. The next day we reached Rhodes and from there sailed on to Patara. ²We found a ship going to Phoenicia, so we got on board and sailed off.

³We came within sight of Cyprus and then sailed south of it on to the port of Tyre in Syria, where the ship was going to unload its cargo. ⁴We looked up the Lord's followers and stayed with them for a week. The Holy Spirit had told them to warn Paul not to go on to Jerusalem. ⁵But when the week was over, we started on our way again. All the men, together with their wives and children, walked with us from the town to the seashore. We knelt on the beach and prayed. ⁶Then after saying good-by to each other, we got into the ship, and they went back home.

⁷We sailed from Tyre to Ptolemais, where we greeted the followers and stayed with them for a day. ⁸The next day we went to Caesarea and stayed with Philip, the preacher. He was one of the seven men who helped the apostles, ⁹and he had four unmarried^a daughters who prophesied.

¹⁰We had been in Caesarea for several days, when the prophet Agabus came to us from Judea. ¹¹He took Paul's belt, and with it he tied up his own hands and feet. Then he told us, "The Holy Spirit says that some of the Jewish leaders in Jerusalem will tie up the man who owns this belt. They will also hand him over to the Gentiles." ¹²After Agabus said this, we and the followers living there begged Paul not to go to Jerusalem.

¹³But Paul answered, "Why are you crying and breaking my heart? I am not only willing to be put in jail for the Lord Jesus. I am even willing to die for him in Jerusalem!"

¹⁴Since we could not get Paul to change his mind, we gave up and prayed, "Lord, please make us willing to do what you want."

ᵃ21.9 *unmarried:* Or "virgin."

Prayer Starter: Dear God, help more and more people to place their faith in Jesus Christ.

Memory Verse: Remember that our Lord Jesus said, "More blessings come from giving than from receiving."

—*Acts 20.35b*

**Paul Speaks
to a Crowd
of People**

The commander told him he could speak, so Paul stood on the steps and motioned to the people. When they were quiet, he spoke to them in Aramaic:

22 "My friends and leaders of our nation, listen as I explain what happened!" ²When the crowd heard Paul speak to them in Aramaic, they became even quieter. Then Paul said:

³I am a Jew, born and raised in the city of Tarsus in Cilicia. I was a student of Gamaliel and was taught to follow every single law of our ancestors. In fact, I was just as eager to obey God as any of you are today.

⁴I made trouble for everyone who followed the Lord's Way,ᵃ and I even had some of them killed. I had others arrested and put in jail. I didn't care if they were men or women. ⁵The high priest and all the council members can tell you that this is true. They even gave me letters to the Jewish leaders in Damascus, so that I could arrest people there and bring them to Jerusalem to be punished.

⁶One day about noon I was getting close to Damascus, when a bright light from heaven suddenly flashed around me. ⁷I fell to the ground and heard a voice asking, "Saul, Saul, why are you so cruel to me?"

⁸"Who are you?" I answered.

The Lord replied, "I am Jesus from Nazareth!"

ᵃ22.4 *followed the Lord's Way:* In the book of Acts, this means to become a follower of the Lord Jesus.

Prayer Starter: Lord, please protect the men and women in the armed forces who are helping protect our country.

Memory Verse: Cheer up! . . .   —*Acts 27.25*

The Plot Against Paul

The next morning more than forty Jewish men got together and vowed that they would not eat or drink anything until they had killed Paul. ¹⁴Then some of them went to the chief priests and the nation's leaders and said, "We have promised God that we would not eat a thing until we have killed Paul. ¹⁵You and everyone in the council must go to the commander and pretend that you want to find out more about the charges against Paul. Ask for him to be brought before your court. Meanwhile, we will be waiting to kill him before he gets there."

¹⁶When Paul's nephew heard about the plot, he went to the fortress and told Paul about it. ¹⁷So Paul said to one of the army officers, "Take this young man to the commander. He has something to tell him."

¹⁸The officer took him to the commander and said, "The prisoner named Paul asked me to bring this young man to you, because he has something to tell you."

¹⁹The commander took the young man aside and asked him in private, "What do you want to tell me?"

²⁰He answered, "Some men are planning to ask you to bring Paul down to the Jewish council tomorrow. They will claim that they want to find out more about him. ²¹But please don't do what they say. More than forty men are going to attack Paul. They have made a vow not to eat or drink anything until they have killed him. Even now they are waiting to hear what you decide."

²²The commander sent the young man away after saying to him, "Don't let anyone know that you told me this."

Prayer Starter: Protect me from all evil.

Memory Verse: Cheer up! I am sure . . .   *—Acts 27.25*

**Agrippa
and
Bernice**

The next day Agrippa and Bernice made a big show as they came into the meeting room. High ranking army officers and leading citizens of the town were also here. Festus then ordered Paul to be brought in ²⁴and said:

King Agrippa and other guests, look at this man! Every Jew from Jerusalem and Caesarea has come to me, demanding for him to be put to death. ²⁵I have not found him guilty of any crime deserving death. But because he has asked to be judged by the Emperor, I have decided to send him to Rome.

26Agrippa told Paul, "You may now speak for yourself." Paul stretched out his hand and said:

²King Agrippa, I am glad for this chance to defend myself before you today on all these charges that my own people have brought against me. ³You know a lot about our religious customs and the beliefs that divide us. So I ask you to listen patiently to me.

Prayer Starter: May the leaders of this world bow down and worship you.

Memory Verse: Cheer up! I am sure that God will do . . . . —*Acts 27.25*

Storm on the Mediterranean

When a gentle wind from the south started blowing, the men thought it was a good time to do what they had planned. So they pulled up the anchor, and we sailed along the coast of Crete. ¹⁴But soon a strong wind called "The Northeaster" blew against us from the island. ¹⁵The wind struck the ship, and we could not sail against it. So we let the wind carry the ship.

¹⁶We went along the island of Cauda on the side that was protected from the wind. We had a hard time holding the lifeboat in place, ¹⁷but finally we got it where it belonged. Then the sailors wrapped ropes around the ship to hold it together. They lowered the sail and let the ship drift along, because they were afraid it might hit the sandbanks in the gulf of Syrtis.

¹⁸The storm was so fierce that the next day they threw some of the ship's cargo overboard. ¹⁹Then on the third day, with their bare hands they threw overboard some of the ship's gear. ²⁰For several days we could not see either the sun or the stars. A strong wind kept blowing, and we finally gave up all hope of being saved.

²¹Since none of us had eaten anything for a long time, Paul stood up and told the men:

You should have listened to me! If you had stayed on in Crete, you would not have had this damage and loss. ²²But now I beg you to cheer up, because you will be safe. Only the ship will be lost.

²³I belong to God, and I worship him. Last night he sent an angel ²⁴to tell me, "Paul, don't be afraid! You will stand trial before the Emperor. And because of you, God will save the lives of everyone on the ship." ²⁵Cheer up! I am sure that God will do exactly what he promised. ²⁶But we will first be shipwrecked on some island!

²⁹The sailors were afraid that we might hit some rocks, and they let down four anchors from the back of the ship. Then they prayed for daylight.

Prayer Starter: Help me to cheer up, Lord, for I believe you will do all you have promised.

Memory Verse: Cheer up! I am sure that God will do exactly . . .
—*Acts 27.25*

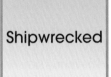

Shipwrecked

The sailors wanted to escape from the ship. So they lowered the lifeboat into the water, pretending that they were letting down an anchor from the front of the ship. ³¹But Paul said to Captain Julius and the soldiers, "If the sailors don't stay on the ship, you won't have any chance to save your lives." ³²The soldiers then cut the ropes that held the lifeboat and let it fall into the sea.

³³Just before daylight Paul begged the people to eat something. He told them, "For fourteen days you have been so worried that you haven't eaten a thing. ³⁴I beg you to eat something. Your lives depend on it. Do this and not one of you will be hurt."

³⁵After Paul had said this, he took a piece of bread and gave thanks to God. Then in front of everyone, he broke the bread and ate some. ³⁶They all felt encouraged, and each of them ate something. ³⁷There were 276 people on the ship, ³⁸and after everyone had eaten, they threw the cargo of wheat into the sea to make the ship lighter.

³⁹Morning came, and the ship's crew saw a coast that they did not recognize. But they did see a cove with a beach. So they decided to try to run the ship aground on the beach. ⁴⁰They cut the anchors loose and let them sink into the sea. At the same time they untied the ropes that were holding the rudders. Next, they raised the sail at the front of the ship and let the wind carry the ship toward the beach. ⁴¹But it ran aground on

a sandbank. The front of the ship stuck firmly in the sand, and the rear was being smashed by the force of the waves.

[42]The soldiers decided to kill the prisoners to keep them from swimming away and escaping. [43]But Captain Julius wanted to save Paul's life, and he did not let the soldiers do what they had planned. Instead, he ordered everyone who could swim to dive into the water and head for shore. [44]Then he told the others to hold on to planks of wood or parts of the ship. At last, everyone safely reached shore.

28 When we came ashore, we learned that the island was called Malta.

Prayer Starter: Thank you for helping us when we are in danger.

Memory Verse: Cheer up! I am sure that God will do exactly what he promised.

—*Acts 27.25*

Paul Bitten by a Snake

The local people were very friendly, and they welcomed us by building a fire, because it was rainy and cold.

³After Paul had gathered some wood and had put it on the fire, the heat caused a snake to crawl out, and it bit him on the hand. ⁴When the local people saw the snake hanging from Paul's hand, they said to each other, "This man must be a murderer! He didn't drown in the sea, but the goddess of justice will kill him anyway."

⁵Paul shook the snake off into the fire and wasn't harmed. ⁶The people kept thinking that Paul would either swell up or suddenly drop dead. They watched him for a long time, and when nothing happened to him, they changed their minds and said, "This man is a god."

¹¹Three months later we sailed in a ship that had been docked at Malta for the winter. The ship was from Alexandria in Egypt and was known as "The Twin Gods."ᵃ ¹²We arrrived in Syracuse and stayed for three days. ¹³From there we sailed to Rhegium. The next day a south wind began to blow, and two days later we arrived in Puteoli. ¹⁴There we found some of the Lord's followers, who begged us to stay with them. A week later we left for the city of Rome.

ᵃ28.11 *known as "The Twin Gods"*: Or "carried on its bow a wooden carving of the Twin Gods." These gods were Castor and Pollux, two of the favorite gods among sailors.

Prayer Starter: Thank you for fish and birds, even for reptiles and insects.

Memory Verse: I am proud of the good news! . . . —*Romans 1.16*

Some of the followers in Rome heard about us and came to meet us at the market of Appius and at the Three Inns. When Paul saw them, he thanked God and was encouraged.

[16]We arrived in Rome, and Paul was allowed to live in a house by himself with a soldier to guard him.

[17]Three days after we got there, Paul called together some of the Jewish leaders and said:

My friends, I have never done anything to hurt our people, and I have never gone against the customs of our ancestors. But in Jerusalem I was handed over as a prisoner to the Romans. [18]They looked into the charges against me and wanted to release me. They found that I had not done anything deserving death. [19]The Jewish leaders disagreed, so I asked to be tried by the Emperor.

But I don't have anything to say against my own nation. [20]I am bound by these chains because of what we people of Israel hope for. That's why I have called you here to talk about this hope of ours. [21]The leaders replied, "No one from Judea has written us a letter about you. And not one of them has come here to report on you or to say anything against you. ²²But we would like to hear what you have to say. We understand that people everywhere are against this new group."

²³They agreed on a time to meet with Paul, and many of them came to his house. From early morning until late in the afternoon, Paul talked to them about God's kingdom. He used the Law of Moses and the Books of the Prophets^a to try to win them over to Jesus.

³⁰For two years Paul stayed in a rented house and welcomed everyone who came to see him. ³¹He bravely preached about God's kingdom and taught about the Lord Jesus Christ, and no one tried to stop him.

^a28.23 *Law of Moses and the Books of the Prophets:* The Jewish Bible, that is, the Old Testament.

Prayer Starter: Dear God, help me be an encouraging friend.

Memory Verse: I am proud of the good news! It is God's powerful way . . .   —*Romans 1.16*

From Paul, a servant of Christ Jesus.

God chose me to be an apostle, and he appointed me to preach the good news ²that he promised long ago by what his prophets said in the holy Scriptures. ³⁻⁴This good news is about his Son, our Lord Jesus Christ! As a human, he was from the family of David.

But the Holy Spiritᵃ proved that Jesus is the powerful Son of God,ᵇ because he was raised from death.

⁵Jesus was kind to me and chose me to be an apostle,ᶜ so that people of all nations would obey and have faith. ⁶You are some of those people chosen by Jesus Christ.

⁷This letter is to all of you in Rome. God loves you and has chosen you to be his very own people.

I pray that God our father and our Lord Jesus Christ will be kind to you and will bless you with peace!

⁸First, I thank God in the name of Jesus Christ for all of you. I do this because people everywhere in the world are talking about your faith. ⁹God has seen how I never stop praying for you, while I serve him with all my heart and tell the good news about his Son.

¹⁰In all my prayers, I ask God to make it possible for me to visit you. ¹¹I want to see you and share with you the same blessings that God's Spirit has given me. Then you will grow stronger in your faith. ¹²What I am saying is that we can encourage each other by the faith that is ours.

¹³My friends, I want you to know that I have often planned to come

for a visit. But something has always kept me from doing it. I want to win followers to Christ in Rome, as I have done in many other places. [14-15]It doesn't matter if people are civilized and educated, or if they are uncivilized and uneducated. I must tell the good news to everyone. That's why I am eager to visit all of you in Rome.

[16]I am proud of the good news! It is God's powerful way of saving all people who have faith, whether they are Jews or Gentiles. [17]The good news tells how God accepts everyone who has faith, but only those who have faith.[d] It is just as the Scriptures say, "The people God accepts because of their faith will live."[e]

[a]1.3,4 *the Holy Spirit:* Or "his own spirit of holiness." [b]1.3,4 *proved that Jesus is the powerful Son of God:* Or "proved in a powerful way that Jesus is the Son of God." [c]1.5 *Jesus was kind to me and chose me to be an apostle:* Or "Jesus was kind to us and chose us to be his apostles." [d]1.17 *but only those who have faith:* Or "and faith is all that matters." [e]1.17 *The people God accepts because of their faith will live:* Or "The people God accepts will live because of their faith."

Prayer Starter: Make me proud of the good news about Jesus, dear God.

Memory Verse: I am proud of the good news! It is God's powerful way of saving all people . . .   *—Romans 1.16*

This Is My Body

Your worship services do you more harm than good. I am certainly not going to praise you for this. [18]I am told that you can't get along with each other when you worship, and I am sure that some of what I have heard is true. [19]You are bound to argue with each other, but it is easy to see which of you have God's approval.

[20]When you meet together, you don't really celebrate the Lord's Supper. [21]You even start eating before everyone gets to the meeting, and some of you go hungry, while others get drunk. [22]Don't you have homes where you can eat and drink? Do you hate God's church? Do you want to embarrass people who don't have anything? What can I say to you? I certainly cannot praise you.

[23]I have already told you what the Lord Jesus did on the night he was betrayed. And it came from the Lord himself.

He took some bread in his hands. [24]Then after he had given thanks, he broke it and said, "This is my body, which is given for you. Eat this and remember me."

[25]After the meal, Jesus took a cup of wine in his hands and said, "This is my blood, and with it God makes his new agreement with you. Drink this and remember me."

[26]The Lord meant that when you eat this bread and drink from this cup, you tell about his death until he comes.

[27]But if you eat the bread and drink the wine in a way that isn't worthy of the Lord, you sin against his body and blood. [28]That's why you must examine the way you eat and drink.

Prayer Starter: Help me be well behaved in church and school, Lord. Help me to respect my teachers.

Memory Verse: I am proud of the good news! It is God's powerful way of saving all people who have faith . . .   *—Romans 1.16*

Paul
Corrects
Peter

James, Peter,[a] and John realized that God had given me the message about his undeserved kindness. And these men are supposed to be the backbone of the church. They even gave Barnabas and me a friendly handshake. This was to show that we would work with Gentiles and that they would work with Jews. [10]They only asked us to remember the poor, and that was something I had always been eager to do.

[11]When Peter came to Antioch, I told him face to face that he was wrong. [12]He used to eat with Gentile followers of the Lord, until James sent some Jewish followers. Peter was afraid of the Jews and soon stopped eating with Gentiles. [13]He and the others hid their true feelings so well that even Barnabas was fooled. [14]But when I saw that they were not really obeying the truth that is in the good news, I corrected Peter in front of everyone and said:

Peter, you are a Jew, but you live like a Gentile. So how can you force Gentiles to live like Jews?

¹⁵We are Jews by birth and are not sinners like Gentiles. ¹⁶But we know that God accepts only those who have faith in Jesus Christ. No one can please God by simply obeying the Law. So we put our faith in Christ Jesus, and God accepted us because of our faith.

¹⁷When we Jews started looking for a way to please God, we discovered that we are sinners too. Does this mean that Christ is the one who makes us sinners? No, it doesn't! ¹⁸But if I tear down something and then build it again, I prove that I was wrong at first. ¹⁹It was the Law itself that killed me and freed me from its power, so that I could live for God.

I have been nailed to the cross with Christ. ²⁰I have died, but Christ lives in me. And I now live by faith in the Son of God, who loved me and gave his life for me.

[a]2.9 *Peter:* The Greek text has "Cephas," which is an Aramaic name meaning "rock."

Prayer Starter: Give me wisdom, Lord, to know when to tell others that they are wrong.

Memory Verse: I am proud of the good news! It is God's powerful way of saving all people who have faith, whether they are Jews or Gentiles.
—*Romans 1.16*

Christ Brings Spiritual Blessings

From Paul, chosen by God to be an apostle of Christ Jesus.

To God's people who live in Ephesus and[a] are faithful followers of Christ Jesus.

2I pray that God our Father and our Lord Jesus Christ will be kind to you and will bless you with peace!

3Praise the God and Father of our Lord Jesus Christ for the spiritual blessings that Christ has brought us from heaven! 4Before the world was created, God had Christ choose us to live with him and to be his holy and innocent and loving people. 5God was kind[b] and decided that Christ would choose us to be God's own adopted children. 6God was very kind to us because of the Son he dearly loves, and so we should praise God.

⁷⁻⁸Christ sacrificed his life's blood to set us free, which means that our sins are now forgiven. Christ did this because God was so kind to us. God has great wisdom and understanding, ⁹and by what Christ has done, God has shown us his own mysterious ways. ¹⁰Then when the time is right, God will do all that he has planned, and Christ will bring together everything in heaven and on earth.

¹¹God always does what he plans, and that's why he appointed Christ to choose us. ¹²He did this so that we Jews would bring honor to him and be the first ones to have hope because of him. ¹³Christ also brought you the truth, which is the good news about how you can be saved. You put your faith in Christ and were given the promised Holy Spirit to show that you belong to God. ¹⁴The Spirit also makes us sure that we will be given what God has stored up for his people. Then we will be set free, and God will be honored and praised.

¹⁵I have heard about your faith in the Lord Jesus and your love for all of God's people. ¹⁶So I never stop being grateful for you, as I mention you in my prayers. ¹⁷I ask the glorious Father and God of our Lord Jesus Christ to give you his Spirit. The Spirit will make you wise and let you understand what it means to know God. ¹⁸My prayer is that light will flood your hearts and that you will understand the hope that was given to you when God chose you. Then you will discover the glorious blessings that will be yours together with all of God's people.

ᵃ1.1 *live in Ephesus and:* Some manuscripts do not have these words. ᵇ1.4,5 *holy and innocent and loving people.* ⁵*God was kind:* Or "holy and innocent people. God was loving ⁵and kind."

Prayer Starter: I praise you, Father, for the spiritual blessings Christ brought from heaven.

Memory Verse: Don't worry . . .   —*Philippians 4.6*

The Armor That God Gives

Finally, let the mighty strength of the Lord make you strong. ¹¹Put on all the armor that God gives, so you can defend yourself against the devil's tricks. ¹²We are not fighting against humans. We are fighting against forces and authorities and against rulers of darkness and powers in the spiritual world. ¹³So put on all the armor that God gives. Then when that evil day[a] comes, you will be able to defend yourself. And when the battle is over, you will still be standing firm.

[14]Be ready! Let the truth be like a belt around your waist, and let God's justice protect you like armor. [15]Your desire to tell the good news about peace should be like shoes on your feet. [16]Let your faith be like a shield, and you will be able to stop all the flaming arrows of the evil one. [17]Let God's saving power be like a helmet, and for a sword use God's message that comes from the Spirit.

[18]Never stop praying, especially for others. Always pray by the power of the Spirit. Stay alert and keep praying for God's people. [19]Pray that I will be given the message to speak and that I may fearlessly explain the mystery about the good news. [20]I was sent to do this work, and that's the reason I am in jail. So pray that I will be brave and will speak as I should.

[21-22]I want you to know how I am getting along and what I am doing. That's why I am sending Tychicus to you. He is a dear friend, as well as a faithful servant of the Lord. He will tell you how I am doing, and he will cheer you up.

[23]I pray that God the Father and the Lord Jesus Christ will give peace, love, and faith to every follower! [24]May God be kind to everyone who keeps on loving our Lord Jesus Christ.

[a]6.13 *that evil day:* Either the present or "the day of death" or "the day of judgment."

Prayer Starter: Help me to stay alert, Lord, and to keep praying for your people.

Memory Verse: Don't worry about anything . . . —*Philippians 4.6*

Timothy and Epaphroditus

My dear friends, you always obeyed when I was with you. Now that I am away, you should obey even more. So work with fear and trembling to discover what it really means to be saved. ¹³God is working in you to make you willing and able to obey him.

¹⁴Do everything without grumbling or arguing. ¹⁵Then you will be the pure and innocent children of God. You live among people who are crooked and evil, but you must not do anything that they can say is wrong. Try to shine as lights among the people of this world, ¹⁶as you hold firmly toᵃ the message that gives life. Then on the day when Christ returns, I can take pride in you. I can also know that my work and efforts were not useless.

[17]Your faith in the Lord and your service are like a sacrifice offered to him. And my own blood may have to be poured out with the sacrifice.[b] If this happens, I will be glad and rejoice with you. [18]In the same way, you should be glad and rejoice with me.

[19]I want to be encouraged by news about you. So I hope the Lord Jesus will soon let me send Timothy to you. [20]I don't have anyone else who cares about you as much as he does. [21]The others think only about what interests them and not about what concerns Christ Jesus. [22]But you know what kind of person Timothy is. He has worked with me like a son in spreading the good news. [23]I hope to send him to you, as soon as I find out what is going to happen to me. [24]And I feel sure that the Lord will also let me come soon.

[25]I think I ought to send my dear friend Epaphroditus back to you. He is a follower and a worker and a soldier of the Lord, just as I am. You sent him to look after me, [26]but now he is eager to see you. He is worried, because you heard he was sick. [27]In fact, he was very sick and almost died. But God was kind to him, and also to me, and he kept me from being burdened down with sorrow.

[28]Now I am more eager than ever to send Epaphroditus back again. You will be glad to see him, and I won't have to worry any longer. [29]Be sure to give him a cheerful welcome, just as people who serve the Lord deserve. [30]He almost died working for Christ, and he risked his own life to do for me what you could not.

[a]2.16 *hold firmly to:* Or "offer them." [b]2.17 *my own blood may have to be poured out with the sacrifice:* Offerings of water or wine were sometimes poured out when animals were sacrificed on the altar.

Prayer Starter: Please help those who are sick, Lord, and keep us well.

Memory Verse: Don't worry about anything, but pray about every-thing. . . .
—*Philippians 4.6*

I Keep on Running

All I want is Christ [9]and to know that I belong to him. I could not make myself acceptable to God by obeying the Law of Moses. God accepted me simply because of my faith in Christ. [10]All I want is to know Christ and the power that raised him to life. I want to suffer and die as he did, [11]so that somehow I also may be raised to life.

[12]I have not yet reached my goal, and I am not perfect. But Christ has taken hold of me. So I keep on running and struggling to take hold of the prize. [13]My friends, I don't feel that I have already arrived. But I forget what is behind, and I struggle for what is ahead. [14]I run toward the goal, so that I can win the prize of being called to heaven. This is the prize that God offers because of what Christ Jesus has done. [15]All of us who are mature should think in this same way. And if any of you think differently, God will make it clear to you. [16]But we must keep going in the direction that we are now headed.

[17]My friends, I want you to follow my example and learn from others who closely follow the example we set for you.

Prayer Starter: Lord, I can hardly wait for the Lord Jesus Christ who is coming again from heaven.

Memory Verse: Don't worry about anything, but pray about everything. With thankful hearts . . .
—*Philippians 4.6*

Be
Glad

Dear friends, I love you and long to see you. Please keep on being faithful to the Lord. You are my pride and joy.

[2]Euodia and Syntyche, you belong to the Lord, so I beg you to stop arguing with each other. [3]And, my true partner,[a] I ask you to help them. These women have worked together with me and with Clement and with the others in spreading the good news. Their names are now written in the book of life.[b]

[4]Always be glad because of the Lord! I will say it again: Be glad. [5]Always be gentle with others. The Lord will soon be here. [6]Don't worry about anything, but pray about everything. With thankful hearts offer up your prayers and requests to God. [7]Then, because you belong to Christ Jesus, God will bless you with peace that no one can completely understand. And this peace will control the way you think and feel.

[8]Finally, my friends, keep your minds on whatever is true, pure, right, holy, friendly, and proper. Don't ever stop thinking about what is truly worthwhile and worthy of praise. [9]You know the teachings I gave you, and you know what you heard me say and saw me do. So follow my example. And God, who gives peace, will be with you.

[a]4.3 *partner:* Or "Syzygus," a person's name.
[b]4.3 *the book of life:* A book in which the names of God's people are written.

Prayer Starter: Help me not to worry about anything, but to pray about everything.

Memory Verse: Don't worry about anything, but pray about everything. With thankful hearts offer up your prayers and requests to God.

—*Philippians 4.6*

The Lord Will Return

My friends, we want you to understand how it will be for those followers who have already died. Then you won't grieve over them and be like people who don't have any hope. ¹⁴We believe that Jesus died and was raised to life. We also believe that when God brings Jesus back again, he will bring with him all who had faith in Jesus before they died. ¹⁵Our Lord Jesus told us that when he comes, we won't go up to meet him ahead of his followers who have already died.

¹⁶With a loud command and with the shout of the chief angel and a blast of God's trumpet, the Lord will return from heaven. Then those who

had faith in Christ before they died will be raised to life. ¹⁷Next, all of us who are still alive will be taken up into the clouds together with them to meet the Lord in the sky. From that time on we will all be with the Lord forever. ¹⁸Encourage each other with these words.

5 I don't need to write you about the time or date when all this will happen. ²You surely know that the Lord's return* will be as a thief coming at night.

ª5.2 *the Lord's return:* The Greek text has "the day of the Lord."

Prayer Starter: Thank you, Lord, for all your promises about the future.

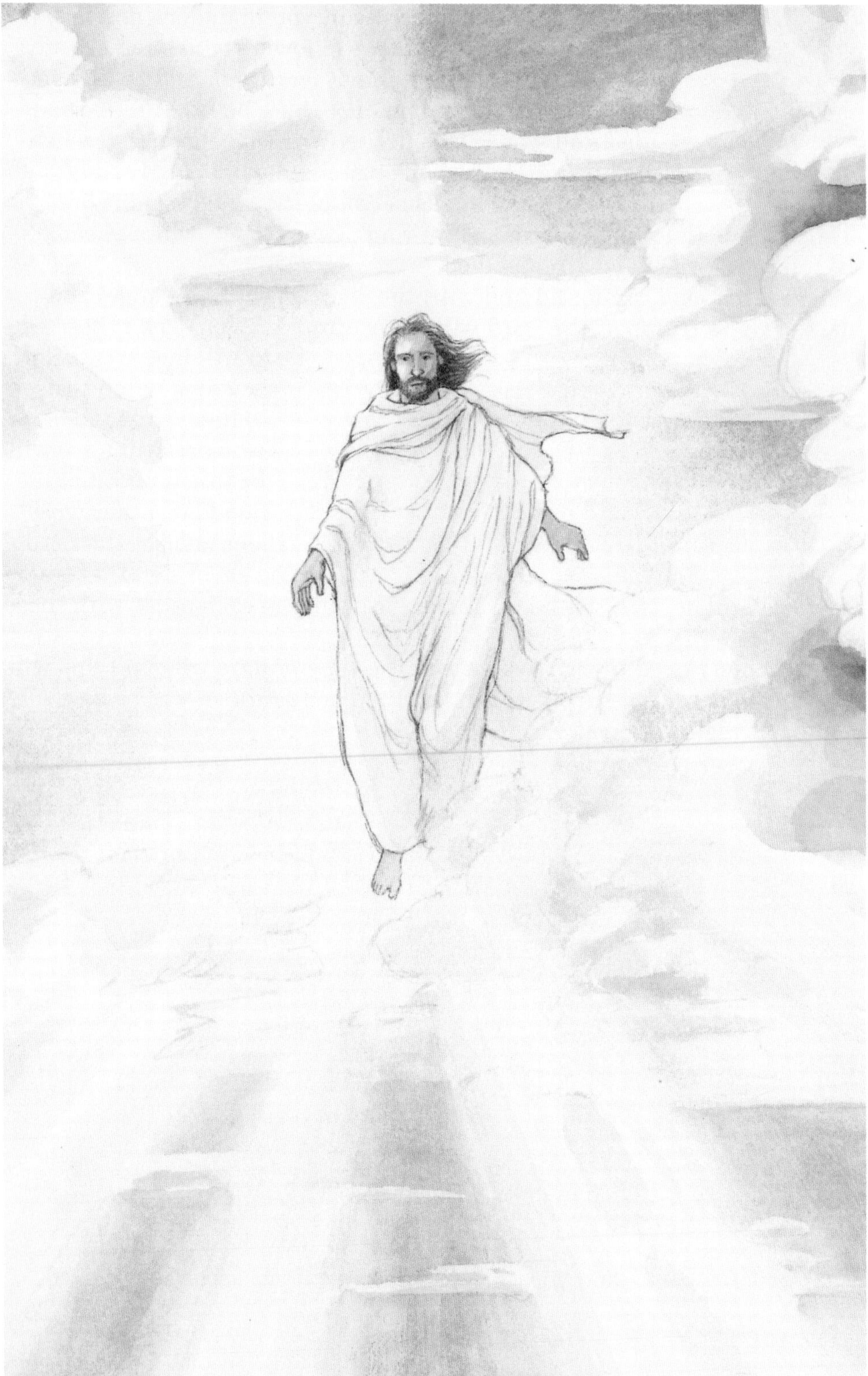

Teach These Things

If you teach these things to other followers, you will be a good servant of Christ Jesus. You will show that you have grown up on the teachings about our faith and on the good instructions you have obeyed. ⁷Don't have anything to do with worthless, senseless stories. Work hard to be truly religious. ⁸⁻⁹As the saying goes,

"Exercise is good for your body,
but religion helps you in every way.
It promises life now and forever."

These words are worthwhile and should not be forgotten. ¹⁰We have put our hope in the living God, who is the Savior of everyone, but especially of those who have faith. That's why we work and struggle so hard.ª

¹¹Teach these things and tell everyone to do what you say. ¹²Don't let anyone make fun of you, just because you are young. Set an example for other followers by what you say and do, as well as by your love, faith, and purity.

¹³Until I arrive, be sure to keep on reading the Scriptures in worship, and don't stop preaching and teaching. ¹⁴Use the gift you were given when the prophets spoke and the group of church leaders[b] blessed you by placing their hands on you. ¹⁵Remember these things and think about them, so everyone can see how well you are doing. ¹⁶Be careful about the way you live and about what you teach. Keep on doing this, and you will save not only yourself, but the people who hear you.

5 Don't correct an older man. Encourage him, as you would your own father. Treat younger men as you would your own brother, ²and treat older women as you would your own mother. Show the same respect to younger women that you would to your sister.

[a]4.10 *struggle so hard:* Some manuscripts have "are treated so badly." [b]4.14 *group of church leaders:* Or "group of elders" or "group of presbyters" or "group of priests."

Prayer Starter: Forgive me, Father, for the times I haven't treated other people nicely.

Memory Verse: You surely know that the Lord's return . . .

—*1 Thessalonians 5.2*

Eunice and Lois

From Paul, an apostle of Christ Jesus.

God himself chose me to be an apostle, and he gave me the promised life that Jesus Christ makes possible.

²Timothy, you are like a dear child to me. I pray that God our Father and our Lord Christ Jesus will be kind and merciful to you and will bless you with peace!

³Night and day I mention you in my prayers. I am always grateful for you, as I pray to the God my ancestors and I have served with a clear conscience. ⁴I remember how you cried, and I want to see you, because that will make me truly happy. ⁵I also remember the genuine faith of your mother Eunice. Your grandmother Lois had the same sort of faith, and I am sure that you have it as well. ⁶So I ask you to make full use of the gift that God gave you when I placed my hands on you.ᵃ Use it well. ⁷God's Spiritᵇ doesn't make cowards out of us. The Spirit gives us power, love, and self-control.

⁸Don't be ashamed to speak for our Lord. And don't be ashamed of

me, just because I am in jail for serving him. Use the power that comes from God and join with me in suffering for telling the good news.

9 God saved us and chose us to be his holy people.
  We did nothing to deserve this,
      but God planned it because he is so kind.
  Even before time began
      God planned for Christ Jesus to show kindness to us.

10 Now Christ Jesus has come to show us the kindness of God.
  Christ our Savior defeated death
      and brought us the good news.
  It shines like a light and offers life that never ends.

11My work is to be a preacher, an apostle, and a teacher.[c] 12That's why I am suffering now. But I am not ashamed! I know the one I have faith in, and I am sure that he can guard until the last day what he has trusted me with.[d] 13Now follow the example of the correct teaching I gave you, and let the faith and love of Christ Jesus be your model. 14You have been trusted with a wonderful treasure. Guard it with the help of the Holy Spirit, who lives within you.

[a]1.6 *when I placed my hands on you:* Church leaders placed their hands on people who were being appointed to preach or teach (see 1 Timothy 4.14). [b]1.7 *God's Spirit:* Or "God." [c]1.11 *teacher:* Some manuscripts add "of the Gentiles." [d]1.12 *what he has trusted me with:* Or "what I have trusted him with."

Prayer Starter: Thank you, God, for all the people who love me.

Memory Verse: You surely know that the Lord's return will be as a thief . . .
—*1 Thessalonians 5.2*

Philemon

Philemon, each time I mention you in my prayers, I thank God. ⁵I hear about your faith in our Lord Jesus and about your love for all of God's people. ⁶As you share your faith with others, I pray that they may come to know all the blessings Christ has given us. ⁷My friend, your love has made me happy and has greatly encouraged me. It has also cheered the hearts of God's people.

⁸Christ gives me the courage to tell you what to do. ⁹But I would rather ask you to do it simply because of love. Yes, as someoneᵃ in jail for Christ, ¹⁰I beg you to help Onesimus!ᵇ He is like a son to me because I led him to Christ here in jail. ¹¹Before this, he was useless to you, but now he is useful both to you and to me.

¹²Sending Onesimus back to you makes me very sad. ¹³I would like to keep him here with me, where he could take your place in helping me while I am here in prison for preaching the good news. ¹⁴But I won't do anything unless you agree to it first. I want your act of kindness to come from your heart, and not be something you feel forced to do.

¹⁵Perhaps Onesimus was taken from you for a little while so that you could have him back for good, ¹⁶but not as a slave. Onesimus is much more than a slave. To me he is a dear friend, but to you he is even more, both as a person and as a follower of the Lord.

¹⁷If you consider me a friend because of Christ, then welcome Onesimus as you would welcome me. ¹⁸If he has cheated you or owes you anything, charge it to my account. ¹⁹With my own hand I write: I, PAUL, WILL PAY YOU BACK. But don't forget that you owe me your life.

ᵃ9 *someone:* Greek "a messenger" or "an old man." ᵇ10 *Onesimus:* In Greek this name means "useful."

Prayer Starter: Lord, use my love to make others happy.

Memory Verse: You surely know that the Lord's return will be as a thief coming . . .
                                              —*1 Thessalonians 5.2*

Faith

Enoch had faith and did not die. He pleased God, and God took him up to heaven. That's why his body was never found. ⁶But without faith no one can please God. We must believe that God is real and that he rewards everyone who searches for him.

⁷Because Noah had faith, he was warned about something that had not yet happened. He obeyed and built a boat that saved him and his family. In this way the people of the world were judged, and Noah was given the blessings that come to everyone who pleases God.

⁸Abraham had faith and obeyed God. He was told to go to the land that God had said would be his, and he left for a country he had never seen. ⁹Because Abraham had faith, he lived as a stranger in the promised land. He lived there in a tent, and so did Isaac and Jacob, who were later given the same promise. ¹⁰Abraham did this, because he was waiting for the eternal city that God had planned and built.

¹³Every one of those people died. But they still had faith, even though they had not received what they had been promised. They were glad just to see these things from far away, and they agreed that they were only strangers and foreigners on this earth. ¹⁴When people talk this way, it is clear that they are looking for a place to call their own. ¹⁵If they had been talking about the land where they had once lived, they could have gone back at any time. ¹⁶But they were looking forward to a better home in

heaven. That's why God wasn't ashamed for them to call him their God. He even built a city for them.

Prayer Starter: Increase my faith, Lord. Help me believe that you are real and that you reward those who seek you.

Memory Verse: You surely know that the Lord's return will be as a thief coming at night.
—*1 Thessalonians 5.2*

Religion That Pleases God

Obey God's message! Don't fool yourselves by just listening to it. ²³If you hear the message and don't obey it, you are like people who stare at themselves in a mirror ²⁴and forget what they look like as soon as they leave. ²⁵But you must never stop looking at the perfect law that sets you free. God will bless you in everything you do, if you listen and obey, and don't just hear and forget.

²⁶If you think you are being religious, but can't control your tongue, you are fooling yourself, and everything you do is useless. ²⁷Religion that pleases God the Father must be pure and spotless. You must help needy orphans and widows and not let this world make you evil.

2 My friends, if you have faith in our glorious Lord Jesus Christ, you won't treat some people better than others. ²Suppose a rich person wearing fancy clothes and a gold ring comes to one of your meetings. And suppose a poor person dressed in worn-out clothes also comes. ³You must not give the best seat to the one in fancy clothes and tell the one who is poor to stand at the side or sit on the floor. ⁴That is the same as saying that some people are better than others, and you would be acting like a crooked judge.

⁵My dear friends, pay attention. God has given a lot of faith to the poor people in this world. He has also promised them a share in his kingdom that he will give to everyone who loves him. ⁶You mistreat the poor. But isn't it the rich who boss you around and drag you off to court? ⁷Aren't they the ones who make fun of your Lord?

⁸You will do all right, if you obey the most important law[a] in the Scriptures. It is the law that commands us to love others as much as we love ourselves. ⁹But if you treat some people better than others, you have done wrong, and the Scriptures teach that you have sinned.

¹⁰If you obey every law except one, you are still guilty of breaking them all. ¹¹The same God who told us to be faithful in marriage also told us not to murder. So even if you are faithful in marriage, but murder someone, you still have broken God's Law.

¹²Speak and act like people who will be judged by the law that sets us free. ¹³Do this, because on the day of judgment there will be no pity for those who have not had pity on others. But even in judgment, God is merciful![b]

¹⁴My friends, what good is it to say you have faith, when you don't do anything to show that you really do have faith? Can that kind of faith save you? ¹⁵If you know someone who doesn't have any clothes or food, ¹⁶you shouldn't just say, "I hope all goes well for you. I hope you will be warm and have plenty to eat." What good is it to say this, unless you do something to help? ¹⁷Faith that doesn't lead us to do good deeds is all alone and dead!

---

[a]2.8 *most important law:* The Greek text has "royal law," meaning the one given by the king (that is, God). [b]2.13 *But even in judgment, God is merciful!:* Or "So be merciful, and you will be shown mercy on the day of judgment."

Prayer Starter: Give me love and concern for those who don't have as much as I have.

Memory Verse: But if we confess our sins . . .   *—1 John 1.9*

You Should
Pray

M y friends, be patient until the Lord returns. Think of farmers who wait patiently for the spring and summer rains to make their valuable crops grow. ⁸Be patient like those farmers and don't give up. The Lord will soon be here! ⁹Don't grumble about each other or you will be judged, and the judge is right outside the door.

¹⁰My friends, follow the example of the prophets who spoke for the Lord. They were patient, even when they had to suffer. ¹¹In fact, we praise the ones who endured the most. You remember how patient Job was and how the Lord finally helped him. The Lord did this because he is so merciful and kind.

¹²My friends, above all else, don't take an oath. You must not swear by heaven or by earth or by anything else. "Yes" or "No" is all you need to say. If you say anything more, you will be condemned.

¹³If you are having trouble, you should pray. And if you are feeling good, you should sing praises. ¹⁴If you are sick, ask the church leadersᵃ to

come and pray for you. Ask them to put olive oil[b] on you in the name of the Lord. [15]If you have faith when you pray for sick people, they will get well. The Lord will heal them, and if they have sinned, he will forgive them.

[16]If you have sinned, you should tell each other what you have done. Then you can pray for one another and be healed. The prayer of an innocent person is powerful, and it can help a lot. [17]Elijah was just as human as we are, and for three and a half years his prayers kept the rain from falling. [18]But when he did pray for rain, it fell from the skies and made the crops grow.

[19]My friends, if any followers have wandered away from the truth, you should try to lead them back. [20]If you turn sinners from the wrong way, you will save them from death, and many of their sins will be forgiven.

[a]5.14 *church leaders:* Or "elders" or "presbyters" or "priests." [b]5.14 *olive oil:* The Jewish people used olive oil for healing.

Prayer Starter: Teach me to sing praises to you, Lord, especially when I am feeling good.

Memory Verse: But if we confess our sins to God . . .   *—1 John 1.9*

186

A Message for Church Leaders

Church leaders,[a] I am writing to encourage you. I too am a leader, as well as a witness to Christ's suffering, and I will share in his glory when it is shown to us.

²Just as shepherds watch over their sheep, you must watch over everyone God has placed in your care. Do it willingly in order to please God, and not simply because you think you must. Let it be something you want to do, instead of something you do merely to make money. ³Don't be bossy to those people who are in your care, but set an example for them. ⁴Then when Christ the Chief Shepherd returns, you will be given a crown that will never lose its glory.

⁵All of you young people should obey your elders. In fact, everyone should be humble toward everyone else. The Scriptures say,

"God opposes proud people,
    but he helps everyone who is humble."

⁶Be humble in the presence of God's mighty power, and he will honor you when the time comes. ⁷God cares for you, so turn all your worries over to him.

⁸Be on your guard and stay awake. Your enemy, the devil, is like a roaring lion, sneaking around to find someone to attack. ⁹But you must resist the devil and stay strong in your faith. You know that all over the world the Lord's followers are suffering just as you are. ¹⁰But God shows undeserved kindness to everyone. That's why he appointed Christ Jesus to choose you to share in his eternal glory. You will suffer for a while, but God will make you complete, steady, strong, and firm. ¹¹God will be in control forever! Amen.

[a]5.1 *Church leaders:* Or "Elders" or "Presbyters" or "Priests."

Prayer Starter: Bless and encourage the pastor of my church, O Lord.

Memory Verse: But if we confess our sins to God, he can always be trusted . . .
                                                        —*1 John 1.9*

God Is Light

The Word that gives life was from the beginning, and this is the one our message is about.

Our ears have heard, our own eyes have seen, and our hands touched this Word.

²The one who gives life appeared! We saw it happen, and we are witnesses to what we have seen. Now we are telling you about this eternal life that was with the Father and appeared to us. ³We are telling you what we have seen and heard, so that you may share in this life with us. And we share in it with the Father and with his Son Jesus Christ. ⁴We are writing to tell you these things, because this makes us^a truly happy.

⁵Jesus told us that God is light and doesn't have any darkness in him. Now we are telling you.

⁶If we say that we share in life with God and keep on living in the dark, we are lying and are not living by the truth. ⁷But if we live in the light, as God does, we share in life with each other. And the blood of his Son Jesus washes all our sins away. ⁸If we say that we have not sinned,

we are fooling ourselves, and the truth isn't in our hearts. ⁹But if we confess our sins to God, he can always be trusted to forgive us and take our sins away.

¹⁰If we say that we have not sinned, we make God a liar, and his message isn't in our hearts.ᵇ

ᵃ1.4 *us:* Some manuscripts have "you." ᵇ1.10 *and his message isn't in our hearts:* Or "because we have not accepted his message."

Prayer Starter: Show me when I sin, Father, so that I can ask for your forgiveness.

Memory Verse: But if we confess our sins to God, he can always be trusted to forgive us . . .   —*1 John 1.9*

On Patmos Island

I am John, a follower together with all of you. We suffer because Jesus is our king, but he gives us the strength to endure. I was sent to Patmos Island,[a] because I had preached God's message and had told about Jesus. [10]On the Lord's day the Spirit took control of me, and behind me I heard a loud voice that sounded like a trumpet. [11]The voice said, "Write in a book what you see. Then send it to the seven churches in Ephesus, Smyrna, Pergamum, Thyatira, Sardis, Philadelphia, and Laodicea."[b]

[12]When I turned to see who was speaking to me, I saw seven gold lampstands. [13]There with the lampstands was someone who seemed to be the Son of Man.[c] He was wearing a robe that reached down to his feet, and a gold cloth was wrapped around his chest. [14]His head and his hair were white as wool or snow, and his eyes looked like flames of fire. [15]His feet were glowing like bronze being heated in a furnace, and his voice sounded like the roar of a waterfall. [16]He held seven stars in his right hand, and a sharp double-edged sword was coming from his mouth. His face was shining as bright as the sun at noon.

[17]When I saw him, I fell at his feet like a dead person. But he put his right hand on me and said:

Don't be afraid! I am the first, the last, [18]and the living one. I died, but now I am alive forevermore, and I have the keys to death and the world of the dead.[d]

[a]1.9 *Patmos Island:* A small island where prisoners were sometimes kept by the Romans. [b]1.11 *Ephesus . . . Laodicea:* Ephesus was in the center with the six other cities forming a half-circle around it. [c]1.13 *Son of Man:* That is, Jesus. [d]1.18 *keys to death and the world of the dead:* That is, power over death and the world of the dead.

Prayer Starter: Help me realize how glorious Jesus Christ really is.

Memory Verse: But if we confess our sins to God, he can always be trusted to forgive us and take our sins away.   —*1 John 1.9*

This is what you must write to the angel of the church in Laodicea:

I am the one called Amen![a] I am the faithful and true witness and the source[b] of God's creation. Listen to what I say.

[15]I know everything you have done, and you are not cold or hot. I wish you were either one or the other. [16]But since you are lukewarm and neither cold nor hot, I will spit you out of my mouth. [17]You claim to be rich and successful and to have everything you need. But you don't know how bad off you are. You are pitiful, poor, blind, and naked.

¹⁸Buy your gold from me. It has been refined in a fire, and it will make you rich. Buy white clothes from me. Wear them and you can cover up your shameful nakedness. Buy medicine for your eyes, so that you will be able to see.

¹⁹I correct and punish everyone I love. So make up your minds to turn away from your sins. ²⁰Listen! I am standing and knocking at your door. If you hear my voice and open the door, I will come in and we will eat together. ²¹Everyone who wins the victory will sit with me on my throne, just as I won the victory and sat with my Father on his throne.

²²If you have ears, listen to what the Spirit says to the churches.

ª3.14 *Amen:* Meaning "Trustworthy." ᵇ3.14 *source:* Or "beginning."

Prayer Starter: Keep me from being lukewarm about you, dear God.

Memory Verse: The one who has spoken these things . . .

—*Revelation 22.20*

The Lamb

In the right hand of the one sitting on the throne I saw a scroll[a] that had writing on the inside and on the outside. And it was sealed in seven places. [2]I saw a mighty angel ask with a loud voice, "Who is worthy to open the scroll and break its seals?" [3]No one in heaven or on earth or under the earth was able to open the scroll or see inside it.

[4]I cried hard because no one was found worthy to open the scroll or see inside it. [5]Then one of the elders said to me, "Stop crying and look! The one who is called both the 'Lion from the Tribe of Judah'[b] and 'King David's Great Descendant'[c] has won the victory. He will open the book and its seven seals."

[6]Then I looked and saw a Lamb standing in the center of the throne that was surrounded by the four living creatures and the elders. The Lamb looked as if it had once been killed. It had seven horns and seven eyes, which are the seven spirits[d] of God, sent out to all the earth.

[7]The Lamb went over and took the scroll from the right hand of the one who sat on the throne. [8]After he had taken it, the four living creatures and the twenty-four elders knelt down before him. Each of them had a harp and a gold bowl full of incense,[e] which are the prayers of God's people. [9]Then they sang a new song,

"You are worthy to receive the scroll and open its seals,
because you were killed.
And with your own blood you bought for God
people from every tribe, language, nation, and race.

[a]5.1 *scroll:* A roll of paper or special leather used for writing on. Sometimes a scroll would be sealed on the outside with one or more pieces of wax. [b]5.5 *'Lion from the Tribe of Judah':* In Genesis 49.9 the tribe of Judah is called a young lion, and King David was from Judah. [c]5.5 *'King David's Great Descendant':* The Greek text has "the root of David" which is a title for the Messiah based on Isaiah 11.1,10. [d]5.6 *the seven spirits:* Some manuscripts have "the spirits." [e]5.8 *incense:* A material that produces a sweet smell when burned. Sometimes it is a symbol for the prayers of God's people.

Prayer Starter: You, Lord, are worthy of all my love and worship.

Memory Verse: The one who has spoken these things says . . .
—*Revelation 22.20*

Worship in Heaven

After this, I saw a large crowd with more people than could be counted. They were from every race, tribe, nation, and language, and they stood before the throne and before the Lamb. They wore white robes and held palm branches in their hands, [10]as they shouted,

"Our God, who sits upon the throne,
has the power to save his people,
    and so does the Lamb."

[11]The angels who stood around the throne knelt in front of it with their faces to the ground. The elders and the four living creatures knelt there with them. Then they all worshiped God [12]and said,

"Amen! Praise, glory, wisdom, thanks, honor, power,
    and strength belong to our God forever and ever! Amen!"

[13]One of the elders asked me, "Do you know who these people are that are dressed in white robes? Do you know where they come from?"
[14]"Sir," I answered, "you must know."
Then he told me:

"These are the ones
    who have gone through the great suffering.
They have washed their robes in the blood of the Lamb
    and have made them white.

Prayer Starter: Amen! Praise, glory, wisdom, thanks, and strength belong to our God forever and ever! Amen!

Memory Verse: The one who has spoken these things says, "I am coming soon!" . . .
            —Revelation 22.20

King of Kings

I looked and saw that heaven was open, and a white horse was there. Its rider was called Faithful and True, and he is always fair when he judges or goes to war. [12]He had eyes like flames of fire, and he was wearing a lot of crowns. His name was written on him, but he was the only one who knew what the name meant.

[13]The rider wore a robe that was covered with[a] blood, and he was known as "The Word of God." [14]He was followed by armies from heaven that rode on horses and were dressed in pure white linen. [15]From his mouth a sharp sword went out to attack the nations. He will rule them with an iron rod and will show the fierce anger of God All-Powerful by trampling the grapes in the pit where wine is made. [16]On the part of the robe that covered his thigh was written, "KING OF KINGS AND LORD OF LORDS."

[17]I then saw an angel standing on the sun, and he shouted to all the birds flying in the sky, "Come and join in God's great feast! [18]You can eat the flesh of kings, rulers, leaders, horses, riders, free people, slaves, important people, and everyone else."

[19]I also saw the beast and all kings of the earth come together. They fought against the rider on the white horse and against his army. [20]But the beast was captured and so was the false prophet.

[a]19.13 *covered with:* Some manuscripts have "sprinkled with."

Prayer Starter: You, O Lord God, are King of kings and Lord of lords.

Memory Verse: The one who has spoken these things says, "I am coming soon!" So, Lord Jesus . . .   *—Revelation 22.20*

Please Come Soon

I saw a new heaven and a new earth. The first heaven and the first earth had disappeared, and so had the sea. ²Then I saw New Jerusalem, that holy city, coming down from God in heaven. It was like a bride dressed in her wedding gown and ready to meet her husband.

³I heard a loud voice shout from the throne:

God's home is now with his people. He will live with them, and they will be his own. Yes, God will make his home among his people. ⁴He will wipe all tears from their eyes, and there will be no more death, suffering, crying, or pain. These things of the past are gone forever.

¹⁰Then with the help of the Spirit, he took me to the top of a very high mountain. There he showed me the holy city of Jerusalem coming down from God in heaven.

¹¹The glory of God made the city bright. It was dazzling and crystal clear like a precious jasper stone.

22 Then I was told:
I am coming soon! And when I come, I will reward everyone for what they have done. ¹³I am Alpha and Omega,ᵃ the first and the last, the beginning and the end.

¹⁶I am Jesus! And I am the one who sent my angel to tell all of you these things for the churches. I am David's Great Descendant,ᵇ and I am also the bright morning star.ᶜ

¹⁷The Spirit and the bride say, "Come!" Everyone who hears thisᵈ should say, "Come!"

If you are thirsty, come! If you want life-giving water, come and take it. It's free!

²⁰The one who has spoken these things says, "I am coming soon!" So, Lord Jesus, please come soon!"

²¹I pray that the Lord Jesus will be kind to all of you.

ᵃ22.13 *Alpha and Omega:* The first and last letters of the Greek alphabet, which sometimes mean "first" and "last." ᵇ22.16 *David's Great Descendant:* The Greek text has "the root of David" which is a title for the Messiah based on Isaiah 11.1,10. ᶜ22.16 *the bright morning star:* Probably thought of as the brightest star. ᵈ22.17 *who hears this:* The reading of the book of Revelation in a service of worship.

Prayer Starter: Lord Jesus, please come soon!

Memory Verse: The one who has spoken these things says, "I am coming soon!" So, Lord Jesus, please come soon!   —*Revelation 22.20*

Subject List

Subject	Page	Passage	Subject	Page	Passage
Abraham (Abram)	182 . . . . . Hebrews 11.5–10, 13–16			175 . . . . . . 1 Thessalonians 4.13—5.2	
				188 . . . . 1 John 1.1–10	
Angels	17 . . . . . . Matthew 2.13–23				
	19 . . . . . . Matthew 4.1–11		Evil Spirits	32 . . . . Mark 1.22–34	
	44 . . . . Luke 1.26–38			33 . . . . Mark 5.1–13	
	96 . . . . Acts 1.3–11			143 . . . . Acts 19.11–20	
	106 . . . . Acts 5.12–26				
	114 . . . . Acts 8.26–35		Faith	23 . . . . Matthew 14.22–36	
	121 . . . . Acts 12.1–19			34 . Mark 5.21–24, 35–42a	
	155 . . . . . Acts 27.13–26, 29			54 . Luke 6.17–18a; 7.1–10	
				56 . . . . Luke 7.36–50	
Animals	33 . . . . Mark 5.1–13			83 . . . . John 11.25–44	
				95 . . . . John 20.19–28	
Bible	177 . . . . 1 Timothy 4.6—5.2			179 . . . . . . 2 Timothy 1.1–14	
				182 . . . . . Hebrews 11.5–10, 13–16	
Blessings (Beatitudes)	20 . . . Matthew 4.25—5.12				
			Fear	23 . . . . Matthew 14.22–36	
Children	37 . . . . Mark 10.2–16			30 . . . . Matthew 26.57–59, 69–74	
Church	25 . . Matthew 16.13–21, 24				
	128 . . . . Acts 15.1–12		Forgiving Others	21 . . . . . . Matthew 6.5–18	
	130 . . . . Acts 15.22–31				
	145 . . . . Acts 20.1–16		Fortune-telling and Witchcraft	113 . . . . Acts 8.9–22	
	191 . . . . Revelation 3.14–22			123 . . . . Acts 13.1–12	
Church Leaders	128 . . . . Acts 15.1–12		Friends	58 . . . . Luke 10.25–37	
	130 . . . . Acts 15.22–31			138 . . . . Acts 18.1–8	
	147 . . . . Acts 20.17–38			160 . . Acts 28.15–23, 30–31	
	187 . . . . 1 Peter 5.1–11			171 . . . . Philippians 2.12–30	
				174 . . . . . . Philippians 4.1–9	
Confessing Our Sins	188 . . . . 1 John 1.1–10			179 . . . . . . 2 Timothy 1.1–14	
				181 . . . . Philemon 4–19	
Devil	19 . . . . . . Matthew 4.1–11				
	123 . . . . Acts 13.1–12		Future Events	96 . . . . Acts 1.3–11	
	169 . . . . Ephesians 6.10–24			173 . . . . Philippians 3.8b–17	
	187 . . . . 1 Peter 5.1–11			175 . . . . . . 1 Thessalonians 4.13—5.2	
Dishonesty	104 . . . . Acts 4.36—5.11			196 . . Revelation 19.11–20a	
				198 . . . . . Revelation 21.1–4, 10–11; 22.12–13, 16–17, 20–21	
Divorce	37 . . . . Mark 10.2–16				
Dreams	17 . . . . . . Matthew 2.13–23		Ghosts	23 . . . . Matthew 14.22–36	
	31 . . . . . Matthew 27.15–26			71 . . . . Luke 24.36–51	
Elijah	185 . . . . James 5.7–20		God Forgives Us	56 . . . . Luke 7.36–50	
Eternal Life	77 . . . . John 3.1–12			167 . . . . . Ephesians 1.1–18	
	78 . . . . John 4.3–14			188 . . . . 1 John 1.1–10	

Memory Verses:
Words to Remember from
God's Word

Here is a complete list of the verses you have been learning as you read this Bible. This is just the beginning of the many wonderful things God has to say to you. Spend time reading and learning more from the Bible every day!

Then after her baby is born, name him Jesus, because he will save his people from their sins.—*Matthew 1.21*

But more than anything else, put God's work first and do what he wants. Then the other things will be yours as well.—*Matthew 6.33*

Jesus healed all kinds of terrible diseases and forced out a lot of demons. But the demons knew who he was, and he did not let them speak.—*Mark 1.34*

Let the children come to me! Don't try to stop them. People who are like these little children belong to the kingdom of God.—*Mark 10.14b*

Jesus became wise, and he grew strong. God was pleased with him and so were the people.—*Luke 2.52*

God will bless everyone who doesn't reject me because of what I do.—*Luke 7.23*

Look at the crows! They don't plant or harvest, and they don't have storehouses or barns. But God takes care of them.—*Luke 12.24*

He told them: "The Scriptures say that the Messiah must suffer, then three days later he will rise from death."—*Luke 24.46*

God loved the people of this world so much that he gave his only Son, so that everyone who has faith in him will have eternal life and never really die.
—*John 3.16*

Jesus then said, "I am the one who raises the dead to life! Everyone who has faith in me will live, even if they die."—*John 11.25*

But the Holy Spirit will come upon you and give you power. Then you will tell about me in Jerusalem, in all Judea, in Samaria, and everywhere in the world.
—*Acts 1.8*

Only Jesus has the power to save! His name is the only one in all the world that can save anyone.—*Acts 4.12*

The Lord's followers who had been scattered went from place to place, telling the good news.—*Acts 8.4*

God is pleased with everyone who worships him and does right, no matter what nation they come from.—*Acts 10.35*

Stop all your dirty talk. Say the right thing at the right time and help others by what you say.—*Ephesians 4.29*

They replied, "Have faith in the Lord Jesus and you will be saved!"—*Acts 16.31a*

Remember that our Lord Jesus said, "More blessings come from giving than from receiving."—*Acts 20.35b*

Cheer up! I am sure that God will do exactly what he promised.—*Acts 27.25*

I am proud of the good news! It is God's powerful way of saving all people who have faith, whether they are Jews or Gentiles.—*Romans 1.16*

Don't worry about anything, but pray about everything. With thankful hearts offer up your prayers and requests to God.—*Philippians 4.6*

You surely know that the Lord's return will be as a thief coming at night.
—*1 Thessalonians 5.2*

But if we confess our sins to God, he can always be trusted to forgive us and take our sins away.—*1 John 1.9*

The one who has spoken these things says, "I am coming soon!" So, Lord Jesus, please come soon!—*Revelation 22.20*